# Cockapoo

understanding and
caring for your breed

Written by
**Stephen Charlton**

# Cockapoo

understanding and
caring for your breed

Written by
**Stephen Charlton**

Pet Book Publishing Company

St. Martin's Farm, Zeals, Warminster, BA12 6NZ, United Kingdom.

Printed and bound in China through Printworks Global, London & Hong Kong.

ISBN: 978-1-906305-85-7
ISBN: 1-906305-85-4


Acknowledgements

The publishers would like to thank Stephen Charlton of Jukee Doodles
Cockapoos for stunning photographs, and the Cockapoo Club of GB for
help and advice. Photos on pages 11, 35, 81, 129, 139, 147, 159, 185 and
192 © Tracy Morgan (www.animalphotographer.co.uk).

# Contents

# Introducing the Cockapoo

Loving, affectionate, bright as a button, the Cockapoo is the designer dog that has it all. Convenient in size, with a chunky but well-balanced body, this is an active dog which has proved to be an outstanding companion, fitting in with a wide variety of lifestyles.

The Cockapoo is a combination of two breeds – a Cocker Spaniel and a Poodle – and he has succeeded in inheriting the very best of this crossbred heritage. He has the keen intelligence of the Poodle, with that special "show off' quality which is a hallmark of the breed. He is also very people orientated and wants nothing more than to be included in all family activities.

From the Cocker Spaniel bloodlines he inherits a merry, even-tempered disposition. He is inquisitive and loves to use his nose, but he also likes to be with

his 'people' and is sweet-natured and affectionate within his family circle. Originally bred as a working gundog, the Cocker Spaniel is biddable which makes him a willing pupil. The clever Cockapoo is also highly trainable. With a bit of work, you will have well-behaved family pet or a successful competitor in canine sports – the choice is yours.

Cockapoos come in a variety of shapes and sizes, depending on their genetic make-up, but with their woolly or wavy coats, drop ears, and twinkling, endearing expression, you will soon come to recognise a Cockapoo when you see one.

## Cockapoo coats

When you see the difference between the tight, curly coat of a Poodle and the flat, silky coat of a Cocker Spaniel, it is not surprising to learn that Cockapoos have different coat types, depending on the genes they have inherited. It is very important to be aware of this before you decide that a Cockapoo is the dog for you, as he may not turn out quite as you imagined.

A Cockapoo coat may be flat, straight, wavy, curly or made up of tight curls. Generally, the flat, straight coat is thicker, and the curlier coats are finer.

*Cockapoo coats range from flat and silky to tight and curly – with lots of variety in-between!*

However, Cockapoos are 'dry' coated, which means you can run your hand through the coat without getting a greasy film on your skin, and this can be beneficial to those with allergies. Bear in mind that it is not always the hair itself that causes an allergic reaction. Allergies are more often triggered by loose hair which is coated in saliva and dander. Unfortunately, the reason why many Cockapoos end up in rescue is because their owners have not tested this out.

*For more information on Cockapoo coats, see page 106.*

## An ideal home

The Cockapoo is a most adaptable dog and, as long as he is with his beloved family, he will think most homes are perfect.

The size of your Cockapoo will depend on the type of Poodle used in his breeding. In most cases, the Toy or the Miniature is used, which gives a height range of between 25 to 35cm (10 to 14in). Even though the Toy Cockapoo is smaller in size, he is still a sturdy little dog and will be able to cope with the rough and tumble of family life, unlike some of the more delicate Toy breeds.

A Cockapoo will be happy as an apartment dweller, and as long as he is well socialised, he will take urban living in his stride. However, he will need to be exercised, so access to green spaces should be considered essential. If you live in the country, a Cockapoo will also suit you down to the ground. A busy, active dog, he will relish the opportunities to free run and use his nose.

If you already have a dog, or you would like to increase your dog pack over time, the Cockapoo will cause no problems. He is out-going and sociable and will enjoy having canine company. With careful supervision in the initial stages, he will also learn to live in harmony with the family cat.

Bear in mind that the Cockapoo is an intelligent dog and you need to allocate time to provide training and mental stimulation. He is the most loving, affectionate and entertaining of dogs, and if you decide to bring a Cockapoo into your life, it is a decision you will never regret.

# The background story

The first Cockapoos were bred in the USA as early as 1950, but it is only in the last ten years that this particular crossbreed has achieved wider popularity. In order to understand the Cockapoo, we need to know what goes into his make up.

## The Poodle

When it comes to 'designer' dogs, Poodles are very often part of the mix, as seen in the number of crossbreeds that include Poodle bloodlines. At the forefront, there is the Labradoodle (Labrador-Poodle) which is probably the most well-established of the crossbreeds, but there are Goldendoodles (Golden Retriever-Poodle), Schnoodles (Schnauzer-

*The Miniature Poodle is regularly used in Cockapoo breeding.*

Poodle), Cavapoos (Cavalier King Charles Spaniel-Poodle), Bichonpoos (Bichon Frise-Poodle), and Yorkiepoos (Yorkshire Terrier-Poodle), to name but a few. So why is the Poodle so much in demand? Let us examine the breed's attributes.

## Coat

The Poodle has a non-shedding wool coat made up of short, thick, curly hair which is very dense and extremely water resistant. But the major bonus is that as the coat is hypoallergenic, meaning it can be tolerated by people who have allergies to dog hair. This was the reason that lay behind creating the first Labradoodle – to provide a guide dog for an allergy sufferer who was blind – and it is why Poodle crossbreeds remain so popular.

However, it is important to bear in mind that coat types vary from crossbreed to crossbreed, and some may be more hypoallergenic than others. To confuse the picture further, different coats will appear within a particular crossbreed, and these different types may even occur in the same litter. So tolerance to dander and saliva needs to be fully investigated before taking on a Poodle crossbreed. For more information, see page 106.

## Size

Poodles comes in three different sizes:

Standard: 55 to 66cm (22 to 26in)

Miniature: 28 to 38cm (11 to 15in)

Toy: 28cm (11in) or under.

The range of sizes means that the Poodle has tremendous versatility when it comes to crossbreeding as it can be matched with other breeds of different sizes.

With Cockapoos, Toy and Miniature Poodles are most commonly used; there are breeders who use Standard Poodles, but they are relatively few and far between.

## Characteristcs and temperament

The Poodle is a highly intelligent dog and is very quick to learn. The Standard Poodle was originally used to retrieve waterfowl in Germany (hence the water-resistant coat), and the two smaller sizes were developed in France where they soon gained a reputation as outstanding companion dogs. The Poodle has a true zest for life, which makes him a joy to own. He is also loving and loyal, and will form a strong bond with his human family.

# Cocker spaniel

The original Cocker Spaniels were developed in England to flush out game. In fact the name 'Cocker' comes from their ability to hunt Woodcock, a wading bird that nests on the ground. During the course of time, the breed has undergone many changes and there are now two distinct breeds, the English Cocker and the American Cocker. To complicate matters further, the show-bred English Cocker is now very different from those bred purely as working dogs. Therefore, the type of Cockapoo you get, both in terms of appearance and temperament, will depend on whether an American Cocker, a show-bred English Cocker, or a working Cocker has been used in the mix.

## English Cocker

Bred to be a working gundog with a strong hunting drive, English Cockers from show lines now look very different from their working cousins.

A show-bred Cocker is a compact, sturdy dog, measuring between 38 and 41cm (15 to 16in) at the shoulder. He has a domed head, long, pendulous ears and a silky coat with abundant feathering which requires a great deal of grooming. He has the merry, equable temperament which is the hallmark of

*Facing page: This English Cocker is from show lines.*

the breed. There is a common misconception that show-bred Cockers are more docile than working Cockers. In reality, show Cockers can be just as busy and energetic as dogs from working lines. They may also be more sensitive and, in some cases, they can be highly strung. In terms of temperament, it is always best to evaluate the individual dogs used for breeding rather than relying on breed stereotypes.

## Working Cocker

Working gundogs are bred for their ability to work in the field, and appearance is therefore of secondary importance, as long as they have the conformation to do the job that is required of them.

In general, a working Cocker is longer in the body and leggier than a Cocker from show lines. The working Cocker's skull is flatter and broader, and his ears are shorter. But most noticeable is the difference in coat – a working Cocker has a short coat that lies flat to the body, and although he will have some feathering, it is minimal compared to his show cousin.

In terms of temperament, the working Cocker has the typically merry, outgoing personality, and is an affectionate companion. He is generally more amenable to living in a larger pack than Cockers from show lines, and this translate well to finding his place in the family pack. This is a dog that thrives on mental stimulation, and he enjoys the opportunity to free run and use his nose.

## Dual Purpose Cocker

This is the result of combining English show Cockers and working Cockers. The combined bloodlines of the two types of Cockers tends to produce a dog with slightly more drive that the purebred show Cocker, and a coat that has feathering but is not as high maintenance as that of the show Cocker.

*A working Cocker: Note the difference in coat and conformation..*

## American Cocker

It is reckoned the first Spaniel travelled to the USA on the Mayflower in 1620, although it was not until 1878 that the first Cocker Spaniel was imported from England and registered with the American Kennel Club. The breed was valued as a formidable worker in the field, and he soon became popular as a show dog and as a companion.

Over time, American-bred Cockers started to look very different from the original English Cockers, and in 1946 they were recognised as a completely separate breed. They are smaller in size – 34 to 39cm (13.5 to 15.5in) – and in the show ring, a domed head with a shorter muzzle is considered highly desirable. The coat is stunning, with extensive silky feathering, which demands very high maintenance. Unfortunately, the American Cocker is not as hale and hearty as the English Cocker, and they are predisposed to a number of inherited health conditions.

As far as temperament is concerned, the American Cocker is a happy and loving companion. For the most part, his working heritage is long forgotten.

## Summing up

So now we have some understanding of the breeds that make up the Cockapoo, we realise why cross breeding is such a complex business and why it takes many generations of breeding to produce a dog that is instantly recognisable as a new 'breed' in terms of both appearance and temperament.

The American Cocker looks very different from the English Cocker and is identified as a breed in its own right.

# Developing
# the Cockapoo

When you examine the history of pedigree dogs breeds, you will discover that often a number of breeds or 'types' have been used during their development. It is only when generation after generation of purebred dogs are mated together, and produce puppies in their own image, that a pedigree breed can be officially recognised.

To the purist, breeding crossbreeds is not highly regarded as it can be seen as no more than combining two breeds, which may produce widely differing offspring. In contrast, the breeder of purebred dogs, is aiming to produce dogs that measure up to the Breed Standard, the written blueprint which describes the 'perfect' specimen.

There are some crossbreeds that have novelty value, and may be no more than a fashion whim,

*Facing page: This is an F1 Cockapoo: His breeding is English Working Cocker crossed with Miniature Poodle.*

but those that have some history, such as the Cockapoo (dating back to 1950) and the Labradoodle (first bred in the late 1980s) have had a chance to establish themselves. They may not be recognised as breeds in their own right, but there are breeders who are campaigning for this status and it is more than likely that official recognition will occur in the fullness of time.

## Understanding crossbreeding

When a Poodle and a Cocker Spaniel are bred together, it is termed a first cross, known as F1. This is the most stable and consistent cross, and offspring will be of a reasonably predictable type in terms of appearance and temperament. They will also have the benefit of hybrid vigour (see page 28) which comes from breeding with two completely unrelated dogs.

However, breeding is never straightforward, and although F1 Cockapoos will be of a similar type, there may be differences between litters, and even between littermates, depending on the pattern of inheritance.

When two F1 Cockapoos are bred together, it is referred to as a second cross and the resulting offspring will be termed F2s. This is more complex and the results are more uncertain, as it is impossible to know which characteristics will come to the fore. Littermates may take on the different traits from their parents – some looking more like Poodles, and some more like Cocker Spaniels. These dogs are termed throwbacks; the phenomenon is also known as the 'grandad effect' relating to this particular mode of inheritance.

Throwbacks are most commonly produced in F2 litters with a fair proportion in F3s, although there will also be offspring which are virtually indistinguishable from F1 Cockapoos. The three variables of Cocker/ Cockapoo/ Poodle continue to crop up within single litters even when breeding extends to four or five generations. However, temperament remains consistent.

When breeding gets to this stage, a lot of homework needs to be done to ensure that there are no shared ancestors within the five-generation pedigree as this may have a detrimental effect on the health of the resulting offspring.

As well as breeding F1 to F1, F2 to F2, and so on, there is also the option of breeding an F1 Cockapoo with a purebred Poodle or Cocker Spaniel. In this instance the resulting offspring are termed F1bs. This form of breeding is used to increase the genetic inheritance of either the Poodle or the Cocker. In most cases, a purebred Poodle is used, as when the resulting puppies are effectively three-quarters Poodle, there is a greater chance of them inheriting the tight, curly, hypoallergenic coat of the Poodle.

However, there are many variables. Cockapoos can vary, looking almost identical to a Cocker or a Poodle, or they may be more of a mix of the two breeds.

## What is hybrid vigour?

This term is closely associated with crossbreeding, When two animals that are genetically different are bred together, the resulting offspring benefit from increased vigour which may relate to physical characteristics, such as size and growth, but they may also show resistance to disease, be relatively free from inherited disorders, and have increased longevity. Obviously this is most apparent in first time crosses, i.e. Poodle to Cocker Spaniel. The effect will be increasingly diluted with multi-generational crosses.

## Cockapoo clubs

The Cockapoo is not recognised by national Kennel Clubs for pedigree dogs, but a number of clubs have been founded on both sides of the Atlantic, dedicated to their development and welfare. They have differing aims, which are outlined below:

Cockapoo Club of GB: Founded in 2011, the Cockapoo Club of GB is the official registration body for Cockapoos in the UK. It promotes the ethical breeding of Cockapoos

*Facing page: An F2 puppy: This term is use when two F1 Cockapoos are bred together.*

in Britain and has approved breeders who are inspected and validated to meet the club's exacting code of ethics. Health testing is a priority and there is also a rehoming scheme. The club has not drawn up a Breed Standard and is not campaigning for official recognition. The aim is to establish a Breeding Standard where health tests are mandatory and temperament is the focus.

Annual events include a Poo Fest, Poo in the Park and the Cockapoo Games, which features a parade of more than 100 Cockapoos of all mixes.

Cockapoo Club of America: This was established in 1999 and a Breed Standard has been drawn up. The focus is on breeding multi-generational Cockapoos, rather than first-time crosses, to promote consistency in type.

American Cockapoo Club: Formed in 2004, this has a different policy; members do not mix generations, and will not breed a Cockapoo back to a Poodle or a Cocker Spaniel. This club has its own Breed Standard.

North American Cockapoo Registry: This organisation, founded in 1999, is working towards breed recognition and provides certification for Cockapoos that are the result of first through to sixth-generation breedings. It declares that... "a true Cockapoo is only a purposeful, planned crossing of a purebred Cocker Spaniel with a purebred Poodle." Their aim is create 'true' Cockapoos for generational breeding.

*The Grandad effect: When F2 Cockapoos are mated, there may be thowbacks. This Cockapoo closely resembles a Cocker and you can see very little of his Poodle ancestry.*

# What should a Cockapoo look like?

There are no set rules when it comes to the appearance of a Cockapoo, so what are breeders striving to attain, and what should potential owners be looking for?

In the world of pedigree dogs, all breeds have their known Breed Standard which is a picture in words describing the perfect specimen in terms of conformation and temperament. This is the guide that is used by breeders to produce typical and healthy animals, and it is also used by judges who evaluate dogs in the show ring.

In the case of the Cockapoo, a crossbreed that is not registered with national Kennel Clubs, there is no accepted Standard which describes what a

*Facing page:*
*This F1 Cockapoo is*
*bred from an English*
*Show Cocker and a*
*Miniature Poodle.*

Cockapoo should look like. In fact, it is unlikely that a Standard will ever be established because of the number of core breeds in the mix, which means that a Cockapoo will never breed 'true'. Cockapoo enthusiasts therefore embrace the variables and do not strive for a single look. However, there are some essentials of the breed which can be considered.

Cockapoos have a keen intelligence and are highly trainable. Out-going and happy, they are very people orientated. They are known for their sweet nature and loyalty.

## Eyes

Large, round, well-set, brown eyes. Typically, the Cockapoo has a look of keen intelligence, but can also look soulful and endearing.

## Ears

Drop ears which frame the face; they may be medium or long in length.

## Tail

In the USA, the tail may be docked, but in the case of the Cockapoo Club of America, the preference is for an undocked tail. In the UK, the tail is always undocked and may be carried straight or curled.

## Coat

Dense, odourless, with little to no shedding. It can have loose curls, or it may be wavy or straight.

## Colour

There are plenty of colours to choose from. The most common are black, white, silver, golden, apricot, red and chocolate, with or without white markings. In addition, Cockapoos have the following patterns and markings:

**Parti:** White with a solid colour.

**Phantom:** Black with brown colouring on the eyebrows and side of the face, on the legs and under the tail.

*Enthusiasts embrace the variables in terms of appearance, but place a high priority on the sweet-natured, biddable temperament which is a hallmark of the best-bred Cockapoos.*

Sable: Black or dark brown at birth, lightening to a mix of gold, silver, red, brown or tan. There are darker points on the face and ears.

Tri-colour: Parti-colour with tan markings over the eyes, on the muzzle, the ears and legs, and sometimes the chest.

Merle: Lighter colours of the base colour swirled with the darker base colour.

Roan: Single white hairs and white patches intermingled with the base colour.

Brindle: The coat has a striped appearance, usually black with a lighter colours which may include tan, cream or brown.

Ticking: Flecks or spots of colour on white areas.

## Size

The size of a Cockapoo will depend on his parentage. English, American and Working Cockers show a slight variation in size, and it depends whether a Toy Poodle, a Miniature or, more unusually, a Standard Poodle is in the mix. The American Cockapoo Club gives the following size categories:

Toy: 25cm (10in) or less, under 5.5kg (12lb).

Miniature: 28-35cm (11-14 in), 5.5-9kg (12-20lb).

**Standard:** 37cm (15in) or higher, over 9kg (20lb).

However, it is worth bearing in mind that when a Toy Poodle is used the resulting offspring may not always be the smallest size of Cockapoo. For example, an American Cocker-Toy Poodle cross (both considered the smallest of the mixes) can produce offspring measuring 37cm (15in), and an English Show Cocker- Miniature Poodle cross can produce Cockapoos of 27cm (11in). So, in fact. actual parental size is the usually the best guide rather then the specific mix of breeds.

*This is an F1 Cockapoo bred from an American Cocker and a Toy Poodle.*

# What do you want from your Cockapoo?

There are hundreds of pedigree dog breeds to choose from, plus a growing number of 'designer' crossbreeds, so how can you be sure that the Cockapoo is the right dog for you? Before you decide on a Cockapoo, you need to be 100 per cent confident that this is the 'breed' that is best suited to your lifestyle.

## Companion

If you want a loyal, affectionate companion that has a special affinity with children, look no further. The Cockapoo relates exceptionally well to people. He is outgoing and friendly with everyone he meets, but he reserves his special love for his family.

The Cockapoo gets on well with children of all ages and, as long as a sense of mutual respect is established, he will be a wonderful entertainer and playmate. He has a sweetness and patience, but he also has lots of get up and go. You will never be bored if you have a Cockapoo in the house!

For those getting on in years, a Cockapoo will provide unstinting love and devotion, and his adaptable nature means that although he needs a reasonable amount of exercise he is not as demanding as many of the sporting/gundog breeds.

## Sports dog

If you want to get involved in one of the canine sports, the Cockapoo could well be the dog for you. He is a highly intelligent. The Cocker Spaniel part of him likes having a job to do, and his Poodle ancestry makes him keen to perform – so take a look at the sports on offer and make your choice.

*For more information, see Opportunities for Cockapoos pages 154*

## Show dog

Remember, the Cockapoo is a crossbreed and is therefore not eligible for exhibiting in the show ring under Kennel Club rules. If you are interested in getting involved in the world of showing, you need to start again and find a pedigree breed that is recognized by your national Kennel Club.

## Therapy dog

Cockapoos are used as assistance dogs, helping those with impaired hearing and as detector dogs, sensing hypolglycemic fluctuations in diabetics. This requires specialised training, but pet owners can get involved in therapy work. This may involve visiting the elderly in residential homes, working with children, or visiting long-stay patients in hospital. The benefits of interacting with dogs are well documented, and the Cockapoo with his affectionate, yet calm nature is an ideal candidate.

There are a number of organisations that train dogs and volunteers for this type of work, and if you decide to get involved, your Cockapoo will enjoy getting lots of attention and you will find the involvement hugely rewarding.

# What does your Cockapoo want from you?

A dog cannot speak for himself, so we need to view the world from a canine perspective and work out what a Cockapoo needs in order to live a happy, contented and fulfilling life.

## Time and commitment

First of all, a Cockapoo needs a commitment that you will care for him for the duration of his life – guiding him through his puppyhood, enjoying his adulthood, and being there for him in his later years. If all potential owners were prepared to make this pledge, there would be scarcely any dogs in rescue.

The Cockapoo loves his own special people and wants nothing more than to be involved in family activities. If he is excluded, or if he is expected to

spend long periods on his own, he will be thoroughly miserable. Cockapoos can suffer from separation anxiety (see page 127), and although you may take steps to prevent this, you must to bear in mind that the Cockapoo needs his people.

If you have to go out to work, or need to be away from home for more than four hours at a stretch, delay dog ownership until your circumstances change.

## Practical matters

The Cockapoo is a relatively easy dog to care for, but you need to take on board his grooming requirements, which will vary depending on coat type. Some coats are high maintenance, others less so, but regular grooming will be needed.

The Cockapoo enjoys his exercise, and he is reasonably good at entertaining himself if you have a well-fenced garden. However, all sizes of Cockapoo benefit from regular outings which give them the opportunity to free-run.

## Leadership

The Cockapoo excels in his role as family companion; he is eager to please and thrives on being the centre of attention. However, you need to bear in mind that a puppy does not arrive in your home knowing how to behave; he has to be guided by his human family so that he learns what you consider to be 'right' and 'wrong'.

This does not mean that you have to be a domineering pack leader or, worse still, try to get your message over with harsh handling. A puppy learns best if you praise and reward the behaviour you want and then he will repeat it in the expectation of more rewards.

It is important not to neglect this aspect of your Cockapoo's education. A happy dog is one that is content with his place in the family circles and understands where the boundaries lie.

*The Cockapoo needs to have his mental and physical energy channelled in a positive direction.*

# Extra considerations

Now you have decided that a Cockapoo is the dog of your dreams, you can narrow your choice so you know exactly what you are looking for.

## Male or female?

Whether you get a male or female Cockapoo comes down to personal preference. Males are a little bigger than females, but this is not of major significance, so it all comes down to temperament.

All Cockapoos are very much individuals in their own right, but there are some gender traits that come to the fore. Most owners agree that the male Cockapoo is more exuberant than the female and remains playful throughout his life. He is very affectionate and is always keen to learn. The female may be a little more reserved; she loves her family but she will give her affection on her own terms. She may decide that there is one special person in the family, and form a particularly strong

bond with that individual. Females also enjoy the chance to use their brains, but may be a little more independent minded than their male counterparts.

If you opt for a female, you will need to cope with her seasons, which will start at any time from six to nine months of age and occur approximately every nine months thereafter. During the three-week period of a season, you will need to keep your bitch away from entire males (males that have not been neutered) to eliminate the risk of an unwanted pregnancy. Some owners also report that females may be a little moody and withdrawn during their seasonal cycle,

Many pet owners opt for neutering, which puts an end to the seasons, and also and has many attendant health benefits. The operation, known as spaying, is usually carried out at some point after the first season. The best plan is to seek advice from your vet.

An entire male may not cause many problems, although some do have a stronger tendency to mark, which could include in the house. However, training will usually put a stop to this. An entire male will also be on the lookout for bitches in season, and this may lead to difficulties, depending on your circumstances.

Neutering (castrating) a male is a relatively simple operation, and there are associated health benefits. Again, you should seek advice from your vet.

## Coat

The Cockapoo has three basic coat types:

- Tight and curly, closely resembling a typical Poodle coat.

- A loose, wavy ringlet coat.

- A straighter coat.

All three coat types can occur in the same litter, and will share similar low-shedding, low-allergen qualities. As already highlighted, there is no guarantee that a Cockapoo will have a hypoallergenic coat; some dogs will be non-shedding, others will shed but to a lesser extent than other breeds. Reduced shedding means less dandruff is produced, which may be an important factor for some allergy sufferers.

If you, or someone in your family, suffers from allergies, the best plan is to find a breeder who will allow you to spend some time with their dogs to monitor reactions. The breeder will give you the benefit of their advice based on their experience, and this will help you to come to a decision.

## Colour

The Cockapoo comes in a wonderful array of colours and, as an added bonus there is considerable variation of shades within each colour. For example, chocolate can fade to a lighter café au lait, and golden Cockapoos can be shades of cream, buff, blonde or champagne. In terms of markings, these can also come in different colours, such as chocolate and blue roans, chocolate and blue merles, black, brown, black and tan or brown and tan phantoms, and parti colours (white with any solid colour). Some patterns and markings are more unusual so you will need to find a breeder that specialises in producing the colours or markings of your choice.

## More than one?

Owning a Cockapoo can be addictive and you may want to expand your dog population. Cockapoos are sociable dogs and will be perfectly happy to share their home with another dog/dogs, but it is important that each dog receives individual care and training, otherwise you will end up with an unruly mob.

Be very wary of a breeder who encourages you to buy two puppies from the same litter, as it is unlikely that the welfare of the puppies is their top priority.

Most responsible breeders have a waiting list of potential purchasers before a litter is even born and have no need to make this type of sale.

If you do decide to take on a second Cockapoo, wait at least 18 months so your first dog is fully trained and settled before embarking on a puppy.

*There are lots of colours to choose from – this Cockapoo puppy is chocolate roan.*

In terms of gender matches, same sex pairs will get on well together, but a male and a female is probably an ideal combination. Obviously if you go ahead with this, one or both dogs will need to ne neutered.

## An older dog

You may decide to miss out on the puppy phase and take on an older dog instead. Such a dog may be harder to track down, but sometimes a breeder will rehome a female when her breeding career is at an end so she will enjoy the benefits of getting more individual attention. In some cases, the breeder may have run on a puppy as potential breeding stock and then found he/she is not suitable for this role, but will still make an excellent pet dog.

There are advantages to taking on an older dog, as you know exactly what you are getting. But the upheaval of changing homes can be quite upsetting, so you will need to have plenty of patience during the settling in period.

## Rehoming a rescued dog

We are fortunate in the fact that Cockapoos are such versatile dogs they rarely have a problem fitting in with their families, and so relatively few end up in rescue. However, there are situations where a family's circumstances change. The reasons are various, ranging from illness or death of the original owner to family breakdown, changing jobs, or even the arrival of a new baby. In the case of the Cockapoo, one of the most common reasons for rehoming is the result of allergy sufferers who have failed to do their homework and then find they cannot tolerate the dog hair/dandruff.

If you decide you want to take on a rescued Cockapoo, try to find out as much as you can about the dog's history so you know exactly what you are taking on. You need to be aware of his age and health status, his likes and dislikes, plus any behavioural issues that may be relevant. You need to be realistic about what you are capable of achieving so you can be sure you can give the dog in question a permanent home.

Regardless of the dog's previous history, you will need to give him plenty of time and be patient with him as he settles into his new home. It may take weeks, or even months before he becomes fully integrated in the family, but if all goes well you will have the reward of knowing that you have given a Cockapoo a second chance.

# Sourcing
# a puppy

# Sourcing
# a puppy

Your aim is to find a healthy Cockapoo puppy that has been reared with the greatest possible care. Where to start?

Tracking down a suitable crossbreed can be more difficult than finding a purebred dog. In the case of pedigree dogs, you can go to dog shows where you can see different examples of your chosen breed which helps you to decide exactly what you want. You have the opportunity to talk to the exhibitors who can give you advice, and they may also have plans for breeding litters in the foreseeable future. You also have the option of contacting your national Kennel Club; KC websites are very informative and give details of breeders and litters.

But with the Cockapoo, a crossbreed that does not have official recognition, you need to be even more careful to do your homework and spend time finding a breeder that produces top-quality, healthy Cockapoos.

## Internet research

The Internet is an excellent resource, but when it comes to finding a puppy, use it with care:

**DO contact a Cockapoo club.**

This is probably the best way of finding a suitable Cockapoo puppy. The club websites have useful information about breeding, training and practical care, and some have a list of breeders that have puppies available. The advantage of going through a club is that members will follow a code of ethics, and this will give you some guarantees regarding breeding stock and health checks.

**DO NOT look at puppies for sale.**

There are legitimate Cockapoo breeders with their own websites, and they may, occasionally, advertise a litter, although in most cases reputable breeders have waiting lists for their puppies. The danger comes from unscrupulous breeders who produce puppies purely for profit, with no thought for the health of the dogs they breed from and no care given to rearing the litter.

This applies particularly to the breeders of so-called designer dogs who may play on your ignorance and offer 'rare' or 'teacup-sized' Cockapoos at inflated prices rather than focusing on producing healthy, typical puppies.

Photos of puppies are hard to resist, but never make

a decision based purely on an advertisement. You need to find out who the breeder is, and have the opportunity to visit their premises and inspect the litter before making a decision.

## Questions, questions, questions

When you find a breeder with puppies available, you will have lots of questions to ask. These should include the following:

- Are you an approved Cockapoo breeder and therefore abide by a code of ethics?

- What size of Poodle has been used in the cross?

- What type of Cocker Spaniel has been used – English, American or working?

- What is the breeding background of the puppies –. are they F1, F2, F3, for example, or are they Cockapoos mated back to a purebred Cocker Spaniel or Poodle (F1bs).

- Where have the puppies been reared? Hopefully they have experienced suitable socialisation in the home environment, to give them the best possible start in life.

- How many are in the litter?

- What is the split of males and females?

- What colours are available?

*Facing page: Find out about as much as you can about how the puppies have been bred and reared.*

- How many have already been spoken for? The breeder may have a waiting list so your choice might be restricted.

- Can I see the mother with her puppies?

- What age are the puppies?

- When will they be ready to go to their new homes?

Bear in mind that puppies need to be with their mother and siblings until they are at least seven weeks of age. Otherwise they miss out on vital learning and communication skills which will have a detrimental effect on them for the rest of their lives.

You should also be prepared to answer a number of searching questions so the breeder can check if you are suitable as a potential owner of one of their puppies.

You will be asked some or all of the following questions:

- What is your home set up?

- Do you have children/grandchildren?

- What are their ages?

- Do you have a securely-fenced garden?

- Is there somebody at home the majority of the time?

- What is your previous experience with dogs?

- Do you already have other dogs at home?

- Do you have plans to compete with your Cockapoo in one of the canine sports?

The breeder is not being intrusive; they need to understand the type of home you will be able to provide in order to make the right match. Do not be offended by this. The breeder is doing it for both the dog's benefit and also for yours.

Steer clear of a breeder who does not ask you questions. He or she may be more interested in making money out of the puppies rather than ensuring that they go to good homes. They may also have taken other short cuts, which may prove disastrous, and very expensive, in terms of vet bills or plain heartache.

## Health issues

As a crossbreed, the Cockapoo benefits from hybrid vigour and has relatively few health related issues. However, they are not exempt from some 'breed' specific disorders and inherited conditions. You therefore need to talk to the breeder about the health status of breeding stock and find out if there are any issues of concern. There are also some health clearances, such as testing for the eye disorder prcd-PRA, which you need to be aware of.

# Puppy watching

A litter of Cockapoo puppies is totally irresistible. Rushing up to greet you, this band of miniature teddy bears all seem to say: "Take me home". However, you must try to put your feelings to one side so that you can make an informed choice.

You need to be 100 per cent confident that the breeding stock is healthy, and the puppies have been reared with love and care, before making a commitment to buy.

## Viewing a litter

It is a good idea to have mental checklist of what to look out for when you visit a breeder. You want to see:

- A clean, hygienic environment.

- Puppies who are out-going, friendly, and eager to meet you.

- A sweet natured mother who is ready to show off her puppies.

- Pups that are well covered, but not pot-bellied (which could be an indication of worms).

- Bright eyes, with no sign of soreness or discharge.

- Clean ears that smell fresh.

- No discharge from the eyes or nose.

- Clean rear ends – matting could indicate upset tummies.

- Lively pups that are keen to play.

It is important that you see the mother with her puppies as this will give you a good idea of the temperament they are likely to inherit. It is also helpful if you can see other close relatives so you can assess the type and temperament that the breeder produces.

In most cases, you will not be able to see the father (sire) as most breeders will travel some distance to find a stud dog that is not too close to their own bloodlines and complements their bitch. However, you should be able to see photos of him and find out how he is bred, which will help you to make an informed decision.

## Companion puppy

In most cases, you will be wanting a Cockapoo purely and simply as a companion, and in this matter, your choice should be guided by the breeder. It is tempting to go for the pup that comes up to you first, or the one that makes you laugh as he chases his siblings. But the breeder will have spent hours and hours watching the puppies as they have developed from newborns. He/she therefore has an in-depth knowledge of how the puppies interact with each other, with other dogs in the family, how they relate to people, and how they cope with new experiences. This is invaluable information when making the right match; the breeder will take into account your family set up and lifestyle and will help you to pick the most suitable puppy.

If you are looking for a dog with a low-allergen coat, make this very clear when you are first in contact with the breeder. It takes a few weeks before the different coat types become apparent, and even then, it takes an expert to make a correct identification.

It is also worth noting that coat and colour do change as a Cockapoo matures. For example:

- A coat which appears soft and straight at birth may change to a wavy/shaggy texture.

- A chocolate made fade to tan, golden or café au lait. Apricot may become cream or buff. Sable starts off very dark and becomes lighter with a more defined coat pattern.

- Hair may lengthen to a loose wave, sometimes with a floppy top-knot.

- A coat can become coarser and curlier in texture.

## Sports puppy

If you have ambitions to compete with your Cockapoo in one of the canine sports, you should discuss this with the breeder. In general Cockapoos love to work; they are intelligent and will adapt well to the task they are asked to perform.

There is an argument for choosing a Cockapoo that has working Cocker Spaniel in his background, as this type tends to have a strong work ethic and be high in energy. However, do not write off Cockapoos with show English Cocker or American Cocker in their bloodlines, as they also have the credentials to be first-class competition dogs.

A good plan is to test each puppy and find out how willing they are to play and interact with you. Try a mini retrieve – maybe just throwing a small toy a short distance and see if the pup is keen to run out and bring it back. If there is a strong desire to play – and to play with you rather than running off with the toy – the chances are that you have the basis of developing a working relationship.

*The breeder will help you to assess temperament.*

# A Cockapoo-friendly home

It may seem an age before your Cockapoo puppy is ready to leave the breeder and move to his new home. But you can fill the time by getting your home ready, and buying the equipment you will need. These preparations apply to a new puppy but, in reality, they are the means of creating an environment that is safe and secure for your Cockapoo throughout his life.

## In the home

Nothing is safe when a puppy is about, and that is undoubtedly true if you have a Cockapoo in the house! Everything is new and exciting for a young puppy; it all needs thorough investigation – and this usually means testing with mouth and teeth.

One thing is certain – a free-ranging Cockapoo puppy cannot be trusted! Remember, it is not only your prized possessions that are under threat; equally relevant is the damage a puppy can inflict on himself. Trailing electric cables are a major hazard so these will need to be secured out of reach. You will need to make sure all cupboards and storage units cannot be opened – or broken into. This applies particularly in the kitchen where you may store cleaning materials, and other substances, which could be toxic to dogs. There are a number of household plants that are poisonous, so these will need to relocated, along with breakable ornaments.

You may decide to declare upstairs off-limits and this is a sensible decision, particularly as negotiating stairs can be hazardous for a young puppy. The best way of doing this is to use a baby gate; these can also be useful if you want to limit your Cockapoo's freedom in any other part of the house. Owners with small children often use a baby gate to make sure that all dog interactions are supervised. This barrier works well, as your dog is separate but does not feel excluded from what is going on.

## In the garden

Cockapoos do not tend to be escape artists, but there is always the exception to the rule so it is better to be safe than sorry. Your garden must be securely fenced; to some extent the height of the fencing depends on the size of Cockapoo, but 1.22m (4 ft) should give you peace of mind. You also need to make sure there are no gaps, as there is always the option of a puppy tunnelling his way out!

Some Cockapoos are enthusiastic gardeners, and will show no respect for your prized plants. It is bad enough to have your garden destroyed, but there is a serious risk that your Cockapoo could be in danger. There are a number of plants that are toxic to dogs so you need to check these out on the internet (www. dogbooksonline.co.uk/caring/poisonous-plants/) and remove them, or limit access to them before your puppy comes home..

Swimming pools and ponds should be covered as most puppies are fearless and, although it is easy for a puppy to take the plunge, it is virtually impossible for him to get out unaided.

You will also need to designate a toileting area. This will assist the house-training process, and it will also make cleaning up easier. For information on house-training, see page?

## House rules

Before your puppy comes home, hold a family conference to decide on the house rules. You need to decide which rooms your puppy will have access to, and establish whether he is to be allowed on the furniture or not. It is important to start as you mean to go on. You cannot invite a puppy on to the sofa for cuddles only to decide in a few months' time that this is no longer desirable.

The Cockapoo is generally an easygoing type, but if his boundaries are uncertain he will be tempted to try his luck. However, if house rules are applied consistently, he will understand what is – and what is not – allowed, and he will learn to respect you and co-operate.

# Buying equipment

There are some essential items of equipment you will need for your Cockapoo. If you choose wisely, much of it will last for many years to come.

*Watch out, nothing is safe when you have a Cockapoo in the house!*

## Indoor crate

Rearing a puppy is so much easier if you invest in an indoor crate. It provides a safe haven for your puppy at night, when you have to go out during the day, and at other times when you cannot supervise him. A puppy needs a base where he feels safe and secure, and where he can rest undisturbed. An indoor crate provides the perfect den, and many adults continue to use them throughout their lives.

Bear in mind the size your Cockapoo will be when he is fully grown, so buy a crate that is large enough for an adult dog. You may not have the same need to keep your Cockapoo out of mischief, but he will still appreciate having his own space where he can find peace and quiet.

You will also need to consider where you are going to locate the crate. The kitchen is usually the most suitable place as this is the hub of family life. Find a snug corner where the puppy can rest when he wants to, but where he can also see what is going on around him, and still be with the family.

## Beds and bedding

The crate will need to be lined with bedding and the best type to buy is synthetic fleece. This is warm and cosy, and as moisture soaks through it, your puppy will not have a wet bed when he is tiny and is still unable to go through the night without relieving himself. This type of bedding is machine washable and easy to dry; buy two pieces, so you have one to use while the other piece is in the wash.

If you have purchased a crate, you may not feel the need to buy an extra bed, although your Cockapoo may like to have a bed in the family room so he feels part of household activities. There is an amazing array of dog-beds to chose from – duvets, bean bags, cushions, baskets, igloos, mini-four posters – so you can take your pick! However, you do need to bear in mind that some beds prove irresistible as far as chewing is concerned, so delay making a major investment until your Cockapoo has outgrown the destructive, puppy phase.

## Collar and lead

You may think that it is not worth buying a collar for the first few weeks, but the sooner your pup gets used to it, the better (see Wearing a collar, page ??). A nylon lightweight collar is recommended, as most puppies will accept it without making a fuss. Be careful when you are fitting the collar that is not too tight, but equally not too loose, as slipping the collar can become a favourite game...

To begin with you will do best with a lightweight lead, making sure it has a secure trigger fastening. As your Cockapoo grows, you may decide to opt for something a little more substantial, depending on your dog's size.

An extending lead can be a useful purchase as you can give your Cockapoo limited freedom when it is not safe or permitted to allow him off lead. However, you should never use it when walking alongside roads as an unexpected pull from your Cockapoo, resulting in the lead extending further than you intended, could have disastrous consequences.

## ID

Your Cockapoo needs to wear some form of ID when he is out in public places. This can be in the form of a disc, engraved with your contact details, attached to the collar. When your Cockapoo is full-grown, you can buy an embroidered collar with your contact details, which eliminates the danger of the disc becoming detached from the collar.

You may also wish to consider a permanent form of ID. Increasingly breeders are having puppies micro-chipped before they go to their new homes. A micro-chip is the size of a grain of rice. It is 'injected' under the skin, usually between the shoulder blades, with a special needle. It has some tiny barbs on it, which dig into the tissue around where it lies, so it does not migrate from that spot.

Each chip has its own unique identification number that can only be read by a special scanner. That ID number is then registered on a national database with your name and details, so that if ever your dog is lost, he can be taken to any vet or rescue centre where he is scanned and then you are contacted.

If your puppy has not been micro-chipped, you can ask your vet to do it, maybe when he goes along for his vaccinations.

## Bowls

Your Cockapoo will need two bowls; one for food, and one for fresh drinking water, which should always be readily available. A stainless steel bowl is a good choice

for a food bowl. Plastic bowls will almost certainly be chewed, and there is a danger that bacteria can collect in the small cracks that may appear.

You can opt for a second stainless steel bowl for drinking water, or you may prefer a heavier ceramic bowl, which will not be knocked over so easily.

## Food

The breeder will let you know what your puppy is eating and should provide a full diet sheet to guide you through the first six months of your puppy's feeding regime – how much they are eating per meal, how many meals per day, when to increase the amounts given per meal and when to reduce the meals per day.

The breeder may provide you with some food when you go and collect your puppy, but it is worth making enquiries in advance about the availability of the brand that is recommended.

## Grooming gear

The amount of grooming equipment you need will depend on your Cockapoo's coat type. Initially, it is worth buying a soft brush, which you can use to accustom your Cockapoo to grooming. As the coat grows, you can add to your grooming kit. For basic care you will need the following:

- Slicker brush: This type of brush has metal pins, which work through the coat.

- Metal comb: A wide-toothed comb is easier to use;

- Nail-clippers: The guillotine type are easy to use.

- Toothbrush and toothpaste: Choose between a long-handled toothbrush or a finger brush, whichever you find easiest. There are flavoured canine toothpastes on the market, which your dog will enjoy.

- Ear wipes: These are easily obtained from most pet shops and generally come in a tub, which is re-sealable to retain moisture.

*The breeder should give you detailed instructions on feeding when you collect your puppy.*

## Toys

Cockapoos love to play, and there is no shortage of dog toys on the market. But before you get carried away with buying a vast range of toys to keep your puppy entertained, you need to think about which are the safest. Plastic toys can be shredded, cuddly toys can be chewed, and toys where the squeaker can be removed should be avoided at all costs. If your Cockapoo ingests part of a toy, it could well result in an internal blockage, and the results of this are often fatal.

The toys to choose should be made of hard rubber; a large, rubber kong which can be stuffed with food is ideal. You can also buy tough, rope tug toys which are virtually indestructible. If you choose any other type of toy, make sure your Cockapoo is always supervised when he is playing with it.

*Make sure toys are suitably robust.*

# Finding a vet

Before your puppy arrives home, you should register with a vet. Visit some the vets in your local area, and speak to other pet owners that you might know, to find out who they recommend. It is so important to find a good vet, almost as much as finding a good doctor for yourself. You need to find someone with whom you can build a good rapport and have complete faith in. Word of mouth is really the best recommendation.

When you contact a veterinary practice, find out the following:

- Does the surgery run an appointment system?

- What are the arrangements for emergency, out-of-hours cover?

- What facilities are available at the practice?

If you are satisfied with what your find, and the staff appear to be helpful and friendly, book an appointment so your puppy can have a health check a couple of days after you collect him.

# Settling in

When you first arrive home with your puppy, be careful not to overwhelm him. You and your family are hugely excited, but the puppy is in a completely strange environment with new sounds, smells and sights. This is a daunting experience, even for the boldest of pups.

Some puppies are very confident, wanting to play straightaway and quickly making friends; others need a little longer. Keep a close check on your Cockapoo's body language and reactions so you can proceed at a pace he is comfortable with.

First, let him explore the garden. He will probably need to relieve himself after the journey home, so take him to the allocated toileting area and, when he performs, give him plenty of praise.

When you take your puppy indoors, let him investigate again. Show him his crate, and encourage him to enter by throwing in a treat. Let him sniff, and allow him to go in and out as he wants to. Later

on, when he is tired, you can put him in the crate while you stay in the room. In this way he will learn to settle and will not think he is being abandoned.

It is a good idea to feed your puppy in his crate, at least to begin with, as this helps to build up a positive association. It will not be long before your Cockapoo sees his crate as his own special den and will go there as a matter of choice. Some owners place a blanket over the crate, covering the back and sides, so that it is even more cosy and den-like.

## Meeting the family

Resist the temptation of inviting friends and neighbours to come and meet the new arrival; your puppy needs to focus on getting to know his new family for the first few days. Try not to swamp your Cockapoo with too much attention. Give him a chance to explore and find his feet. There will be plenty of time for cuddles later on!

If you have children in the family, you need to keep everything as calm as possible. Cockapoos seem to have a natural affinity with children, but they have to learn how to behave around them, particularly if you have small children. It is very easy for a puppy to become over-excited by raised voices, or by children running around and behaving unpredictably, and this can easily lead to mouthing and nipping.

The best plan is to get the children to sit on the floor
and give them all a treat. Each child can then call
the puppy, stroke him, and offer a treat. In this way
the puppy realizes that it is not a free for all, and that
he needs to interact with each child calmly
and sensibly in order to get his treat.

If he tries to nip or mouth, make
sure there is a toy at the ready, so
his attention can be diverted to
something he is allowed to bite.
If you do this consistently, he will
learn to inhibit his desire to mouth
when he is interacting with people.

Right from the start, impose a
rule that the children are not
allowed to pick up or carry the
puppy. They can cuddle him
when they are sitting on
the floor.

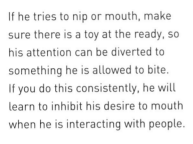

This may sound a little severe, but a wriggly puppy can be dropped in an instant, sometimes with disastrous consequences. If possible, try to make sure your Cockapoo is only given attention when he has all four feet on the ground. Cockapoos can be over-exuberant, particularly as youngsters, so if your pup learns that jumping up is not rewarding, it will pay dividends later on.

Involve all family members with your puppy's day-to-day care; this will enable the bond to develop with the whole family as opposed to just one person. Encourage the children to train and reward the puppy, teaching him to follow their commands without question.

## The animal family

Cockapoos get on well with other dogs, but if you have a resident dog it is important to supervise early interactions to ensure that relations get off on the right footing.

Your adult dog may be allowed to meet the puppy at the breeder's, which is ideal as the older dog will not feel threatened if he is away from home. But if this is not possible, allow your dog to smell the puppy's bedding (the bedding supplied by the breeder is fine) before they actually meet so he familiarizes himself with the puppy's scent.

The garden is the best place for introducing the puppy, as the adult will regard it as neutral territory. He will probably take a great interest in the puppy and sniff him all over. Most puppies are naturally submissive in this situation, and your pup may lick the other dog's mouth or roll over on to his back. Try not to interfere as this is the natural way that dogs get to know each other.

You will only need to intervene if the older dog is too boisterous, and alarms the puppy. In this case, it is a good idea to put the adult on his lead so you have some measure of control.

It rarely takes long for an adult to accept a puppy, as he does not constitute a threat. This will be underlined if you make a big fuss of the older dog so that he has no reason to feel jealous. But no matter how well the two dogs are getting on, do not leave them alone unless one is crated.

## Feline friends

The Cockapoo has an outgoing friendly nature, and although he will be fascinated by the family cat to begin with, it will not take long to establish harmonious relations. Cockapoos do not have a strong prey drive, but a moving cat is a big temptation so your Cockapoo must learn right from the start that cats are not for chasing. You will need to supervise early interactions and progress step by step, making sure the pair are never left alone together until their relationship is fully established. This is an on-going process but all the time your Cockapoo is learning that he is rewarded for ignoring the cat. In time, the novelty will wear off and the pair will live in peace. Indeed, many a Cockapoo has become best friends with the family cat, and some have even ended up sharing a bed!

## Feeding

The breeder will generally provide enough food for the first few days so the puppy does not have to cope with a change in diet – and possible digestive upset – along with all the stress of moving home.

Some puppies eat up their food from the first meal onwards, others are more concerned by their new surroundings and are too distracted to eat. Do not worry unduly if your puppy seems disinterested in his food for the first day or so. Give him 10 minutes to eat what he wants and then remove the leftovers and start afresh at the next meal. Obviously if you have any concerns about your puppy in the first few days, seek advice from your vet.

Cockapoos are not the most food orientated of dogs and some lose interest in their food bowl very quickly. It may help if you feed your Cockapoo in his crate where he will not be so easily distracted and can eat in peace. If you have children, you need to establish a rule that no one is to go near the dog when he is feeding. This is sound commonsense, and removes all risk of problems arising, no matter how unintentional they may be.

However, you should also work at your Cockapoo's food manners so he never feels threatened when he is eating and does not feel protective of his food bowl. You can do this by giving him half his ration, and then dropping food around his bowl. This will stop him guarding his bowl and, at the same time, he will see your presence in a positive light. You can also call him away from the bowl and reward him with some food – maybe something extra special – which he can take from your hand.

Start doing this as soon as your puppy arrives in his new home, and continue working on it throughout his life.

## The first night

Your puppy will have spent the first weeks of his life with his mother or curled up with his siblings. He is then taken from everything he knows as familiar, lavished with attention by his new family – and then comes bed time when he is left all alone. It is little wonder that he feels abandoned.

The best plan is to establish a night-time routine, and then stick to it so that your puppy knows what is expected of him. Take your puppy into the garden to relieve himself, and then settle him in his crate. Some people leave a low light on for the puppy at night for the first week, others have tried a radio as company or a ticking clock. A covered hot-water bottle, filled with warm water, can also be a comfort. Like people, puppies are all individuals and what works for one, does not necessarily work for another, so it is a matter of trial and error.

Be very positive when you leave your puppy on his own; do not linger, or keep returning; this will make the situation more difficult. It is inevitable that he will protest to begin with, but if you stick to your routine, he will accept that he gets left at night – but you always return in the morning.

## Rescued dogs

Settling an older, rescued dog in the home is very similar to a puppy in as much as you will need to make the same preparations regarding his homecoming. As with a puppy, an older dog will need you to be consistent, so start as you mean to go on.

There is often an initial honeymoon period when you bring a rescued dog home, where he will be on his best behaviour for the first few weeks. It is after these first couple of weeks that the true nature of the dog will show, so be prepared for subtle changes in his behaviour. It may be advisable to register with a reputable training club, so you can seek advice on any training or behavioural issues at an early stage.

Above all, remember that a rescued dog ceases to be a rescued dog the moment he enters his forever home and should be treated like any other family pet.

*Can you give a Cockapoo a second chance of a forever home?*

# House training

This is an aspect of training that first-time owners dread, but if you start as you mean to go on, it will not be long before your Cockapoo understands what is required.

The key to successful house training is vigilance and consistency. If you establish a routine, and you stick to it, your puppy will understand what is required. Equally, you must be there to supervise him at all times – except when he is safely tucked up in his crate. It is when a puppy is left to wander from room to room that accidents are most likely to happen.

As discussed earlier, you will have allocated a toileting area in your garden already. You need to take your puppy to this area every time he needs to relieve himself so he builds up an association and knows why you have brought him out to the garden.

Establish a routine and make sure you take your puppy out at the following times:

- First thing in the morning

- After mealtimes

- On waking from a sleep

- Following a play session

- Last thing at night.

A puppy should be taken out to relieve himself every two hours as an absolute minimum. If you can manage an hourly trip out, so much the better. The more often your puppy gets it 'right', the quicker he will learn to be clean in the house. It helps if you use a verbal cue, such as "busy", when your pup is performing and, in time, this will trigger the desired response.

Do not put your puppy out on the doorstep in the hope that he will toilet on his own. Most pups simply sit there, waiting to get back inside the house! No matter how bad the weather is, accompany your puppy and give him lots of praise when he performs correctly.

Do not rush back inside as soon as he has finished. Your puppy might start to delay in the hope of prolonging his time outside with you. Praise him, have a quick game – and then you can both return indoors.

## When accidents happen

No matter how vigilant you are, there are bound to be accidents. If you witness the accident, take your puppy outside immediately, and give him lots of praise if he finishes his business out there.

If you are not there when he has an accident, do not scold him when you discover what has happened. He will not remember what he has done and will not understand why you are cross with him. Simply clean it up and resolve to be more vigilant next time.

Make sure you use a deodoriser, available in pet stores, when you clean up, ,otherwise your pup will be drawn to the smell and may be tempted to use the same spot again.

# Choosing
# a diet

There are so many different types of dog food on sale – all claiming to be the best – so how do you know what is likely to suit your Cockapoo?

When choosing a diet, there are basically three categories to choose from:

## Complete

This is probably the most popular diet as it is easy to feed and is specially formulated with all the nutrients your dog needs. This means that you should not add any supplements or you may upset the nutritional balance. Most complete diets come in different life stages: puppy, adult maintenance and senior, so this means that your Cockapoo is getting what he needs when he is growing, during adulthood, and as he becomes older. You can even get prescription diets for dogs with particular health issues.

Generally, an adult maintenance diet should contain 21-24 per cent protein and 10-14 per cent fat. Protein levels should be higher in puppy diets, and reduced in veteran diets. Cockapoos can be prone to skin allergies, so it is advisable to opt for a diet that is based on natural ingredients. Avoid diets with a high proportion of grain or cereal as they are used purely as bulking agents and serve no nutritional purpose.

## Canned/pouches

This type of food, known as wet food, is usually fed with hard biscuit, and most Cockapoos find it very appetizing. However, the ingredients – and the nutritional value – do vary significantly between the different brands so you will need to check the label. The more natural wet foods contain rice rather than other cereals containing gluten, so select this type to avoid allergic reactions.

Bear in mind that wet foods, as their name indicates, often have a high moisture content, so you need to be sure your Cockapoo is getting all the nutrition he needs.

## Homemade

There are some owners who like to prepare meals especially for their dogs – and it is probably much appreciated. The danger is that although the food is tasty, and your Cockapoo may appreciate the variety, you cannot be sure that it has the correct nutritional balance.

If this is a route you want to go down, you will need to find out the exact ratio of fats, carbohydrates, proteins, minerals and vitamins that are needed, which is quite an undertaking.

The Barf (Biologically Appropriate Raw Food) diet is another, more natural approach to feeding, and may work well with dogs that have skin conditions resulting from a food allergy. Dogs are fed a diet mimicking what they would have eaten in the wild, consisting of raw meat, bone, muscle, fat, and vegetable matter.

There are now a number of companies that specialise in producing the Barf diet in frozen form, which will make your job a lot easier.

*You need to find a diet that matches your Cockapoo's age and lifestyle.*

## Feeding regime

When your puppy arrives in his new home he will need four meals, evenly spaced throughout the day. You may decide to keep to the diet recommended by your puppy's breeder, and if your pup is thriving there is no need to change. However, if your puppy is not doing well on the food, or you have problems with supply, you will need to make a change.

When switching diets, it is very important to do it on a gradual basis, changing over from one food to the next, a little at a time, and spreading the transition over a week to 10 days. This will avoid the risk of digestive upset.

When your puppy is around 12 weeks, you can cut out one of his meals; he may well have started to leave some of his food indicating he is ready to do this. By six months, he can move on to two meals a day – a regime that will suit him for the rest of his life.

## Faddy feeders

As already observed, the Cockapoo is not passionate about his food and so there is the very real danger that you may start trying to tempt his appetite. One look from those dark eyes is enough to melt your heart, stirring you to greater efforts to find a food that your Cockapoo will really like. At first you may add some gravy, then you may try some chicken... The Cockapoo is far from stupid, and he will quickly realize that if he holds out, tastier treats will follow.

This is a bad game to play as not only will you run out of tempting delicacies, you will also be losing your Cockapoo's respect.

If your Cockapoo is turning up his nose at mealtimes, give him 10 minutes to eat what he wants, and then take up his bowl and give him fresh food at his next mealtime. Do not feed him treats in between meals. If you continue this regime for a couple of days, your Cockapoo will realize that there is no percentage in holding out for better food as it never materializes.

In most cases, this is just a 'trying it on' phase, and if you cope with commonsense, you will soon return to the status quo and your Cockapoo will be content with his normal rations.

If, however, your dog refuses all food for more than 24 hours you need to observe his behaviour to see if there are any signs of ill health, which may involve the need for a veterinary check up.

## Bones and chews

Puppies love to chew, and many adults also enjoy gnawing on a bone. A raw marrow bone is ideal, but make sure it is always given under supervision.

Nylon bones are also a favourite with Cockapoos. They come in a variety of sizes and flavours, and some have raised nodules which are excellent for keeping teeth clean.

Rawhide chews are best avoided; it is all too easy for a Cockapoo to bite off a chunk and swallow it, with the danger of it then causing a blockage.

## Ideal weight

In order to help to keep your Cockapoo in good health it is necessary to monitor his weight. As a breed, Cockapoos are not prone to obesity as they are not greedy dogs, but there are always exceptions to the rule. A dog that is carrying too much weight is vulnerable to many health issues; he has a poorer quality of life as he cannot exercise properly, and he will almost certainly have a reduced life expectancy.

When judging your Cockapoo's condition, look at him from above, and make sure you can see a definite 'waist'. You should be able to feel his ribs, but not see them.

If you are concerned about your Cockapoo's weight, get into the habit of visiting your veterinary surgery on a monthly basis so that you can weigh him. You can keep a record of his weight so you can make adjustments if necessary.

If you are concerned that your Cockapoo is putting on too much weight, or equally if you think he is underweight, consult your vet, who will help you to plan a suitable diet.

# Caring for your Cockapoo

The Cockapoo is not a difficult dog to care for and exercise. Grooming is a different matter, and this will entirely depend on your Cockapoo's coat type.

# Coat care

As already highlighted, the Cockapoo can have one of three basic coat types. This will be evident within a few weeks of birth so, hopefully, the breeder has given you sufficient guidance to know what you are getting.

When a Cockapoo puppy arrives in his new home, he will not need much in the way of grooming, regardless of coat type. However, it is important to get your pup used to being handled. This will stand him in good stead if he grows a high maintenance coat, and even if his adult grooming needs are going to be relatively straightforward, this aspect of his care should not be neglected.  A grooming session gives you the opportunity to check your dog and to discover any minor problems, such as sore places, or any abnormalities, such as lumps and bumps which may need to be investigated. Remember, if you spot a problem early on, you increase the chance of an early diagnosis and successful treatment.

The first step is to get your puppy used to being handled so that he accepts the attention without resentment. Initially, he will wriggle and attempt to mouth you, but just ignore his protests. Hold him steady for a few moments, and reward him when he is still. A puppy needs to learn that it is OK to be touched all over; if you fail to do this, he may try to warn you off by growling, which could develop into more problematic behaviour.

Start by handling your puppy all over, stroking him from his head to his tail. Lift up each paw in turn, and reward him with a treat when he co-operates. Then roll him over on to his back and tickle his tummy; this is a very vulnerable position for a dog to adopt, so do not force the issue. Be firm but gentle, and give your Cockapoo lots of praise when he does as you ask.

The adult coat comes through when a Cockapoo is around eight months of age; the most obvious sign is that mats start appearing in the topcoat and in the soft undercoat. The amount of matting varies depending on coat type, but it will mostly be seen in the beard, ears, collar area, legs, undercarriage, and tail. From this point you will need to adapt your grooming regime depending on coat type:

## Straight coat

This is the easiest coat to care for and, in most cases, it can be kept at its natural length. However, it will need regular brushing with a ball-pin brush at least three of four times a week to prevent tangles and mats forming.

Trimming is not essential but most owners use thinning scissors to cut back the long hair that grows on the fringe and over the eyes. The beard may also need to be tidied up as it can get soiled after a Cockapoo has been eating, and it can get pretty soggy when he has had a drink!

## Wavy coat with loose ringlets

This type of coat can look spectacular if it is kept at full length, but it is no easy matter. The majority of owners opt for a smart teddy bear trim (see page 111) which can be done every three months if you want to keep the coat short, or every six months if you can cope with a little more grooming between trims.

If you allow the coat to grow to its full length, you need to be prepared to devote a lot of time to grooming. Daily brushing and combing should become part of your routine to keep the coat mat and tangle-free. But twice a year the coat will shed over a two-week period, and then you will really have your work cut out. You will know when the moult is happening as you will be able to feel the matting of the undercoat through the long hairs, and it is not easy to get through to the skin.

The moulted undercoat needs to be removed, and the only way to do this is by wetting the coat. If you attempt to do it when the coat is dry, the hair frizzes

*Facing page: The amount of grooming your Cockapoo needs depends on coat type.*

up and you will break and damage the hair as well as ending up with an afro-style Cockapoo!

You will need to work through the coat stage by stage:

- First thoroughly wet the coat using a diluted coat conditioner.

- Start at the paws and work upwards, line grooming the entire coat. You need to use a rake and an 8 or 10 blade tool for this, grooming from root to tip, which will loosen the undercoat.

- Then use a flexible brush to dislodge the coat. This is done by gently teasing it down the long, wet hair shaft. Once you have worked through the coat, you will need to give it a thorough rinse to get rid of all traces of conditioner.

- Allow the coat to dry naturally, or you can use a hairdryer and 'scrunch dry' using your fingers. Do not brush the coat when it is drying or you will end up with a wild, hairy coat rather than the beautiful loose ringlets that are such a feature of this coat.

- If you are keeping your Cockapoo in full coat, it is advisable to trim along the line of the undercarriage as this hair can become very dirty and hard to manage.

## Tight, curly coat

It really is a mission impossible to keep this type of coat at full length as it mats so easily. Therefore, owners opt for a teddy bear trim, which needs to be done every three months by a professional groomer.

As well as clipping, the coat will need to be groomed, using a ball pin or slicker brush on a regular basis to keep it in good order.

There are different styles of teddy bear trim:

**Classic Teddy Bear:** Clippers or scissors can be used for this trim, depending on the length of coat you desire. It is better to use scissors if you want a longer length coat; a clipped coat will generally be around 3 to 4cm long, and this is easier to maintain. The aim is to achieve a rounded teddy bear shape, with longer hair on the legs; the ears will also be trimmed to a rounded shape.

**Lamb Cut:** This is similar to the trim used for Poodles, and gives a short, easy-to-care-for coat. The coat on the body is short and the hair on the muzzle, face and feet is also clipped short.

**Cocker Spaniel Show Cut:** This is designed along the lines of the coat seen on a show Cocker. The top of the body is clipped short; the coat on the sides of the body is left longer A crest of hair may be left on

Coat type can vary
between littermates –
the pup (pictured left) is
straight-coated.

top of the head, although the areas around the eyes, ears and fringe are cut short so you can see the facial features.

## Professional groomers

Some Cockapoo owners become expert groomers and prefer to do the job themselves rather than employing the services of a professional groomer. However, if this is not a task you wish to undertake, there are plenty of professionals to choose from. The best plan is to get a recommendation from your Cockapoo's breeder if they live locally, or talk to other owners (contactable through Cockapoo clubs) and find a reputable groomer in your area.

Check out the following:

- The groomer's qualifications. You also need to find out if they have experience with Cockapoos.

- The premises – are they clean, hygienic and dog friendly?

- Most importantly, talk to the groomer, and perhaps ask if you can watch them at work so you are confident that your dog will be treated with sensitivity and kindness.

# Routine care

In addition to grooming, you will need to carry out some routine care.

## Eyes

Check the eyes for signs of soreness or discharge. You can use a piece of cotton wool (cotton) – a separate piece for each eye – and wipe away any debris. If your Cockapoo has long hair around his eyes, keep this trimmed to avoid the hair brushing against the eyeball, causing damage or discomfort.

## Ears

The ears should be clean and free from odour. You can buy specially-manufactured ear wipes, or you can use a piece of cotton wool to clean them if necessary. Do not probe into the ear canal or you risk doing more harm than good.

Some Cockapoos grow hair inside the ear canal, which can cause problems with trapped ear wax. This hair will therefore need to be plucked out, using finger and thumb. You can buy a powder which will help you to grip the hair and make the job easier. If in doubt, ask your vet.

## Teeth

Dental disease is increasing among dogs so teeth cleaning should be seen as an essential part of your care regime. The build up of tartar on the teeth can result in tooth decay, gum infection and bad breath, and if it is allowed to accumulate, you may have no option but to get the teeth cleaned under anaesthetic.

When your Cockapoo is still a puppy, accustom him to teeth cleaning so it becomes a matter of routine. Dog toothpaste comes in a variety of meaty flavours, which your Cockapoo will like, so you can start by putting toothpaste on your finger and gently rubbing his teeth. You can then progress to using a finger brush or a toothbrush, whichever you find most convenient.

Remember to reward your Cockapoo when he co-operates and then he will positively look forward to his teeth-cleaning sessions.

## Nails

Nail trimming is a task dreaded by many owners – and many dogs – but, again, if you start early on, your Cockapoo will get used to the task you have to perform and will not fight against it.

If your dog has white nails, you will be able to see

*Facing page: A Cockapoo thrives on a regime of regular, varied exercise.*

the quick (the vein that runs through the nail), which you must avoid at all costs. If you cut the quick it will bleed profusely and cause considerable discomfort. Obviously, the task is much harder in dark nails as you cannot see the quick. The best policy is to trim little and often so the nails don't grow too long, and you do not risk cutting too much and catching the quick.

If you are worried about trimming your Cockapoo's nails, go to your vet so you can see it done properly. If you are still concerned, you can always use the services of a professional groomer.

## Exercise

The Cockapoo thrives on having a busy, interesting life and exercise should be seen as an essential part of his daily routine. It is important to bear in mind that exercise meets both mental and physical needs. He needs to be kept fit and active, but he also needs the stimulation of exploring new places, investigating different smells, and the opportunity to meet and greet new friends – human and canine.

When a Cockapoo is growing, exercise needs to be limited, particularly in the larger size crosses, as joints are vulnerable while a dog is still growing. Playing in the garden will be sufficient to begin with, stepping up to short outings on lead, with the opportunity to let off steam, free running for 10 minutes or so.

Once your Cockapoo is adult, try to factor in a least one 30 minute walk a day, which can be a combination of lead walking and free running. If you have a larger dog, he will appreciate two walks a day – and he will be more than happy to accompany you on longer treks when you have some free time.

Swimming is an excellent form of exercise which most Cockapoos seem to enjoy – particularly if a game of retrieve is involved. If you allow your dog to swim, make sure you choose a safe stretch of water where there is easy access in and out.

## Playing games

This is a great way of providing physical exercise and mental stimulation. Cockapoos are naturally playful, and the more you interact, the more rewarding it will be for both of you.

The Cockapoo's spaniel ancestry means that he is a natural hunter/retriever, and so games that involve searching and retrieving will come easily to him. Most Cockapoos are eager to retrieve a toy or a ball (make sure the ball is big enough so it cannot be swallowed) and this is a good game to play if you have limited time for exercise.

If your Cockapoo has a favourite toy you can hide it, either in one room in the house, or in the garden, and send him off to search for it. The Cockapoo has a busy, inquisitive nature, and he will keep at a task until he has the reward of finding his toy.

If your Cockapoo is not motivated by toys, you can play the same game but hide food in parts of the garden and allow your dog to sniff it out. In fact, you can, on occasion, scatter the contents of your dog's food bowl over a confined area and then allow him to search for it. This is a hugely rewarding exercise for your Cockapoo – and he will keep going until he has found every last morsel!

## The older Cockapoo

One of the great benefits of owning a crossbreed is that they generally have a very good life expectancy. Most Cockapoos will make it to their early to mid teens – and a few even exceed this.

However, it is inevitable that your Cockapoo will slow up as he gets older, and you need to keep a close check to monitor when this change occurs as it will vary from dog to dog. The older Cockapoo may sleep more and he may be reluctant to go for longer walks. He may show signs of stiffness when he gets up from his bed, but these generally ease when he starts moving. Some older Cockapoos may have impaired vision, and some may become a little deaf, but as long as their senses do not deteriorate dramatically, this is something older dogs learn to live with.

If you treat your older dog with kindness and consideration, he will enjoy his later years and suffer the minimum of discomfort. It is advisable to switch him over to a senior diet, which is more suited to his needs, and you may need to adjust the quantity, as he will not be burning up the calories as he did when he was younger and more energetic. Make sure his sleeping quarters are warm and free from draughts, and if he gets wet, make sure you dry him thoroughly.

Most important of all, be guided by your Cockapoo. He will have good days when he feels up to going for a walk, and other days when he would prefer to potter in the garden. If you have a younger dog at home, this may stimulate your Cockapoo to take more of an interest in what is going on, but make sure he is not pestered as he needs to rest undisturbed when he is tired.

## Letting go

Inevitably there comes a time when your Cockapoo is not enjoying a good quality of life, and you need to make the painful decision to let him go. We would all wish that our dogs died, painlessly, in their sleep but, unfortunately, this is rarely the case.

However, we can allow our dogs to die with dignity, and to suffer as a little as possible, and this should be our way of saying thank you for the wonderful companionship they have given us.

When you feel the time is drawing close, talk to your vet who will be able to make an objective assessment of your Cockapoo's condition and will help you to make the right decision.

This is the hardest thing you will ever have to do as a dog owner, and it is only natural to grieve for your beloved Cockapoo. But eventually, you will be able to look back on the happy memories of times spent together, and this will bring much comfort. You may, in time, feel that your life is not complete without a Cockapoo, and you will feel ready to welcome a new puppy into your home.

*Be especially considerate to your Cockapoo as he enters old age.*

# Social skills

To live in the modern world, without fear and anxieties, your Cockapoo needs to receive an education in social skills so that he learns to cope calmly and confidently in a wide variety of situations. The Cockapoo is an out-going dog, with few hang-ups, and will relish the opportunity to broaden his horizons.

## Early learning

The breeder will have begun a programme of socialisation by getting the puppies used to all the sights and sounds of a busy household. You need to continue this when your pup arrives in his new home, making sure he is not worried by household equipment, such as the vacuum cleaner or the washing machine, and that he gets used to unexpected noises from the radio and television.

To begin with, your puppy needs to get used to all the members of his new family (see Meeting the Family, page 84), but then you should give him the opportunity to meet friends and other people that come to the house. If you do not have children of your own, make sure your puppy has the chance to meet and play with other people's children – making sure interactions are always supervised – so he learns that humans come in small sizes, too.

## Home alone

The Cockapoo adores his human family and his best thing is to be with them. For most of the time, this is the lifestyle he can expect, but there are times when he has to be left at home on his own. Obviously these periods will be limited – a maximum of four hours should be your guiding rule – but you need to be confident that your Cockapoo can cope with this without becoming anxious. Cockapoos are so attached to their owners, there is a real danger of them developing separation anxiety and becoming highly distressed – and possibly destructive – if they have to cope on their own.

To counteract this, you must teach your puppy that it is fine to spend time alone. Feed him in his crate and then wait before you let him out. If he is in his crate overnight, don't rush to let him out first thing in the morning; wait a few minutes and allow him to hear you moving around before you go to him.

When you do let your Cockapoo out of his crate, do not make a big fuss. Speak to him calmly, tell him he has been good, and continue with your everyday business. Adopt the same approach when you leave the house. Settle your dog in his crate – ideally with a kong filled with food which will give him an occupation – and don't make a performance of saying goodbye to him. Make sure your first few outings away from home are relatively short, and when you return, be calm and sensible as you free your Cockapoo from his crate.

Gradually build up the length of time you leave your Cockapoo. In this way, he will learn to settle on his own. He will understand that he spends time on his own – but you always return.

## The outside world

When your puppy has completed his vaccinations, he is ready to venture into the outside world. Cockapoos are generally confident but there is a lot for a youngster to take on board, so do not swamp him with too many new experiences when you first set out.

Obviously you need to work at lead-training (see page 138) before you set out on your first expedition. There will be plenty of distractions to cope with, so you do not want additional problems of coping with a dog that is pulling or lagging on the lead.

So, hopefully, you can set off with your Cockapoo walking by your side on a loose lead. He may need additional encouragement when you venture further afield, so arm yourself with some extra special treats, which will give him a good reason to focus on you when required!

Start socializing your puppy in a quiet area with light traffic, and only progress to a busier place when he is ready. There is so much to see and hear – people (maybe carrying bags or umbrellas), pushchairs, bicycles, cars, lorries, machinery – so give your puppy a chance to take it all in.

If he does appear worried, do not fall into the trap of sympathizing with him, or worse still, picking him up. This will only teach your pup that he had a good reason to be worried and, with luck, you will 'rescue' him if he feels scared.

Instead, give a little space so he does not have to confront whatever he is frightened of, and distract him with a few treats. Then encourage him to walk past, using a positive tone of voice, never forcing him by yanking on the lead. Reward him for any forward movement, and your puppy will soon learn that he can trust you, and there is nothing to fear.

Your pup also needs to continue his education in canine manners, started by his mother and by his littermates, as he needs to be able to greet all dogs calmly, giving the signals that say he is friendly and offers no threat. If you have a friend who has a dog of sound temperament, this is an ideal way to get your puppy used to social interactions. As he gets older and more established, you can widen his circle of canine acquaintances.

*The time you spend socialising your Cockapoo is invaluable.*

## Training classes

A training class will give your Cockapoo the opportunity to work alongside other dogs in a controlled situation, and he will also learn to focus on you in a different, distracting environment. Both these lessons will be vital as your dog matures.

However, the training class needs to be of the highest calibre or you risk doing more harm than good. Before you go along with your puppy, attend a class as an observer to make sure you are happy with what goes on.

Find out the following:

- How much training experience do the instructors have?

- Are the classes divided into appropriate age categories?

- Do they use positive, reward-based training methods?

If the training class is well run, it is certainly worth attending. Both you and your Cockapoo will learn useful training exercises. It will increase his social skills, and you will have the chance to talk to lots of like-minded dog enthusiasts.

# Training guidelines

The Cockapoo is a clever dog and is quick to learn. He will enjoy training sessions as he likes to use his brain, but make sure you keep them rewarding so your Cockapoo enjoys spending quality time with you.

You will be keen to get started, but in your rush to get training underway, do not neglect the fundamentals that could make the difference between success and failure. You need to get into the mindset of a Cockapoo, working out what motivates him and, equally, what makes him switch off. Decide on your priorities for training, set realistic targets, and then think of ways of making your training as positive, and as fun, as possible.

When you start training, try to observe the following guidelines:

- Choose an area that is free from distractions so your puppy will focus on you. You can move on to a more challenging environment as your pup progresses.

- Do not train your puppy just after he has eaten or when you have returned from exercise. He will either be too full, or too tired, to concentrate.

- Do not train if you are in a bad mood, or if you are short of time – these sessions always end in disaster!

- Providing a worthwhile reward is an essential tool in training. You may need to find some extra special food treats, such as cheese or cooked liver, or you may do better with finding a toy your Cockapoo really values.

- If you decide to use a toy, make sure it is only brought out for training sessions so that it accrues added value.

- Keep your verbal cues simple, and always use the same one for each exercise. For example, when you ask your puppy to go into the Down position, the cue is "Down", not "Lie Down", Get Down", or anything else. Remember your Cockapoo does not speak English; he associates the sound of the word with the action.

- If your dog is finding an exercise difficult, break it down into small steps so it is easier to understand.

- Do not make your training sessions boring and repetitious. Your Cockapoo will lose concentration and will cease to co-operate.

- Do not train for too long, particularly with a young puppy that has a very short attention span, and always end training sessions on a positive note. This does not necessarily mean getting an exercise right. If your pup is tired and making mistakes, ask him to do a simple exercise so you have the opportunity to praise and reward him. You may well find that he benefits from having a break and will make better progress next time you try.

- Remember that if a Cockapoo is rewarded for a behaviour, he is likely to repeat it – so make sure you are 100 per cent consistent and always reward the 'right' behaviour.

# First lessons

Like all puppies, a young Cockapoo will soak up new experiences like a sponge, so training should start from the time your pup arrives in his new home.

## Wearing a collar

You may, or may not, want your Cockapoo to wear a collar all the time. But when he goes out in public places he will need to be on a lead, and so he should be used to the feel of a collar around his neck. The best plan is to accustom your pup to wearing a soft collar for a few minutes at a time until he gets used to it.

Fit the collar so that you can get at least two fingers between the collar and his neck. Then have a game to distract his attention. This will work for a few moments; then he will stop, put his back leg up behind his neck and scratch away at the peculiar itchy thing round his neck, which feels so odd.

Bend down, rotate the collar, pat him on the head and distract him by playing with a toy or giving him a treat. Once he has worn the collar for a few minutes each day,

he will soon ignore it and become used to it.

Remember, never leave the collar on your puppy unsupervised, especially when he is outside in the garden, or when he is in his crate, as it is could get snagged, causing serious injury.

## Walking on the lead

This is a simple exercise, but the Cockapoo can be a dog in a hurry, so it is a good idea to master the basics, and for your Cockapoo to learn good lead walking manners before problems with pulling arise.

- Once your puppy is used to the collar, take him outside into your secure garden where there are no distractions.

- Attach the lead and, to begin with, allow him to wander with the lead trailing, making sure it does not become snagged. Then pick up the lead and follow the pup where he wants to go; he needs to get used to the sensation of being attached to you.

- The next stage is to get your Cockapoo to follow you, and for this you will need some treats. To give yourself the best chance of success, make sure the treats are high value – cheese, sausage or cooked liver – so your Cockapoo is motivated to work with you.

- Show him you have a treat in your hand, and then encourage him to follow you. Walk a few paces, and if he is walking with you, stop and reward him. If he puts on the brakes, simply change direction and lure him with the treat.

- Next introduce some changes of direction so your puppy is walking confidently alongside you. At this stage, introduce a verbal cue "Heel" when your puppy is in the correct position.

- You can then graduate to walking your puppy outside the home – as long as he has completed his vaccination programme – starting in quiet areas and building up to busier environments.

*A Cockapoo that walks on the lead without pulling ahead or lagging behind is a pleasure to own.*

## Training strategy

Some Cockapoos decide that pulling on the lead is a good option, and, in no time, the dog is taking you for a walk. This soon becomes an unpleasant experience and it is important to adopt a strategy so that your Cockapoo realizes there is absolutely no percentage in pulling.

Restrict lead training to the garden in the initial stages so you are working in an environment that is free from distractions.

Walk a few paces, being very aware of any tension on the lead. If you feel the lead tighten and your Cockapoo is attempting to get ahead of you, stop, change direction, and set off again. Your Cockapoo needs to understand that pulling ahead has exactly the opposite effect to that which he wants. Rather than calling the tune, he has to co-operate with you.

Keep a good supply of tasty treats and remember only reward – with food and with verbal praise – when he is walking on a loose lead by your side. The mistake made by many owners at this stage is to use the treats to lure the dog into position rather than rewarding him for the correct behaviour.

Keep training sessions short, and when you are ready to venture into the outside world, do not be too ambitious to begin with. Build up the level of distraction and the duration of lead walking only when your Cockapoo is consistently showing the behaviour you want.

# Come when called

The Cockapoo is utterly devoted to his family, but there are times when he gets distracted. There are so many enticing smells, places to explore, people and dogs to meet...

The Cockapoo has an excellent sense of smell and when he picks up a scent, he may become deaf to your calls. In this situation it is so easy to shout at your dog or, worse still, you may get so fed up with him that you limit his free running exercise. This would be a great shame as it will have a severe impact on your Cockapoo's quality of life, and walks for you will become a chore rather than one of the great pleasures of owning a dog.

Your aim must be to make yourself as exciting as possible so that coming when called is even more rewarding than following a scent. This will need to be built up over a period of time, with lots of repetition, so

your Cockapoo sees you as a fun person that is always ready to reward him.

Hopefully, the breeder will have laid the foundations simply by calling the puppies to "Come" at mealtimes, or when they are moving from one place to another.

You can build on this when your puppy arrives in his new home, calling him to "Come" when he is in a confined space, such as the kitchen. This is a good place to build up a positive association with the verbal cue – particularly if you ask your puppy to "Come" to eat his dinner!

The next stage is to transfer the lesson to the garden. Arm yourself with some treats, and wait until your puppy is distracted. Then call him, using a higher-pitched, excited tone of voice. At this stage, a puppy wants to be with you, so capitalise on this and keep practising the verbal cue, rewarding your puppy with a treat and lots of praise when he comes to you.

Now you are ready to introduce some distractions. Try calling him when someone else is in the garden, or wait a few minutes until he is investigating a really interesting scent. When he responds, make a really big fuss of him and give him some extra treats so he knows it is worth his while to come to you. If your puppy responds, immediately reward him with a treat.

If he is slow to come, run away a few steps and then call again, making yourself sound really exciting. Jump up and down, open your arms wide to welcome him; it doesn't matter how silly you look, he needs to see you as the most fun person in the world.

When you have a reliable recall in the garden, you can venture into the outside world. Do not be too ambitious to begin with; try a recall in a quiet place with the minimum of distractions so you can be assured of success.

Do not make the mistake of only asking your dog to come at the end of his allotted exercise period. What is the incentive in coming back to you if all you do is clip on his lead, marking the end of his free time? Instead, call your dog at random times, giving him a treat and a stroke, and then letting him go free again. In this way, coming to you – and focusing on you – is always rewarding.

# Stationary exercises

## Sit

The best method is to lure your Cockapoo into position, and for this you can use a treat or his food bowl.

Hold the reward (a treat or food bowl) above his head. As he looks up, he will lower his hindquarters and go into a sit.

Practice this a few times and when your puppy understands what you are asking, introduce the verbal cue, "Sit".

When your Cockapoo understands the exercise, he will respond to the verbal cue alone, and you will not need to reward him every time he sits. However, it is a good idea to give him a treat on a random basis when he co-operates to keep him guessing!

## Down

This is an important lesson, and can be a lifesaver if an emergency arises and you need to bring your Cockapoo to an instant halt.

You can start with your dog in a Sit or a Stand for this exercise. Stand or kneel in front of him and show him you have a treat in your hand. Hold the treat just in front of his nose and slowly lower it towards the ground, between his front legs.

As your Cockapoo follows the treat he will go down on his front legs and, in a few moments, his hindquarters will follow. Close your hand over the treat so he doesn't cheat and get the treat before he is in the correct position. As soon as he is in the Down, give him the treat and lots of praise.

Keep practising, and when your Cockapoo understands what you want, introduce the verbal cue "Down".

*With practice, your Cockapoo will go into the Down on a verbal cue.*

# Control exercises

## Wait

This exercise teaches your Cockapoo to "Wait" in position until you give the next command. It differs from the Stay exercise, where he must stay where you have left him for a more prolonged period. The most useful application of "Wait" is when you are getting your dog out of the car and you need him to stay in position until you clip on his lead.

Start with your puppy on the lead to give you a greater chance of success. Ask him to "Sit", then stand in front him. Step back one pace, holding your hand, palm flat, facing him. Wait a second and then come back to stand in front of him. You can then reward him and release him with a word, such as "OK".

Practise this a few times, waiting a little longer before you reward him, and then introduce the verbal cue "Wait".

You can reinforce the lesson by using it in different situations, such as asking your Cockapoo to "Wait" before you out his food bowl down.

## Stay

You need to differentiate this exercise from the Wait by using a different hand signal and a different verbal cue.

Start with your Cockapoo in the Down, as he is most likely to be secure in this position. Stand by his side and then step forwards, with your hand held back, palm facing the dog.

Step back, release him, and then reward him. Practise until your Cockapoo understands the exercise and then introduce the verbal cue "Stay".

Gradually increase the distance you can leave your puppy, and increase the challenge by walking around him – and even stepping over him – so that he learns he must "Stay" until you release him.

## Leave

A response to this verbal cue means that your Cockapoo will learn to give up a toy on request, and it follows that he will give up anything when he is asked, which is very useful if he has got hold of a forbidden object. This not simply a matter of obeying the verbal cue to "Leave"; it is establishing the status quo where you are the decision-maker and your Cockapoo is ready to co-operate with you.

- The "Leave" command can be taught quite easily when you are first playing with your puppy. As you gently take a toy from his mouth, introduce the verbal cue, "Leave", and then praise him.

- If he is reluctant, swap the toy for another toy or a treat. This will usually do the trick.

- Do not try to pull the toy from his mouth if he refuses to give it up, as you will make the situation confrontational. Let the toy go 'dead' in your hand, and then swap it for a new toy, or a really high-value treat so this becomes the better option.

- Remember to make a big fuss of your Cockapoo when he does as you ask so that he learns that co-operation is always the best – and most rewarding – option.

# Opportunities for Cockapoos

A fun day out for dogs and their owners, organised by the Cockapoo Club of Great Britain.

# Opportunities for Cockapoos

The Cockapoo is a clever, versatile dog and will thrive on training challenges. Make sure he is sufficiently motivated so working is never a chore, and focus on building a great partnership which will enrich your relationship with your dog.

## Good Citizen Scheme

The Kennel Club Good Citizen Scheme was introduced to promote responsible dog ownership, and to teach dogs basic good manners. In the US there is one test; in the UK there are four award levels: Puppy Foundation, Bronze, Silver and Gold.

Exercises within the scheme include:

- Walking on lead

- Road walking

- Control at door/gate.

- Food manners

- Recall

- Stay

- Send to bed

- Emergency stop.

## Competitive obedience

This is a sport where you are assessed as a dog and handler, completing a series of exercises including heelwork, recalls, retrieves, stays, sendaways and scent discrimination.

The Cockapoo is more than capable of competing in this discipline, but make sure training is fun, and you do not put too much pressure on your dog. The Obedience exercises are relatively simple to begin with, involving heelwork, a recall and stays in the lowest class, and, as your progress through, more exercises are added, and the aids you are allowed to give are reduced.

To achieve top honours in this discipline requires intensive training as precision and accuracy are of paramount importance. However, you must guard against drilling your Cockapoo, as he will quickly lose motivation.

## Agility

The Cockapoo is a natural at this sport, and if you get your dog focused on the equipment, you will be amazed at his speed – and his enthusiasm!

In Agility, the dog completes an obstacle course under the guidance of his owner. You need a good element of control, as the dog completes the course off the lead.

In competition, each dog completes the course individually and is assessed on both time and accuracy. The dog that completes the course with the fewest faults, in the fastest time, wins the class. The obstacles include an A-frame, a dog-walk, weaving poles, a seesaw, tunnels, and jumps.

Classes are divided into size categories; Cockapoos will be classified as Small or Medium.

## Rally O

If you do not want to get involved in the rigours of Competitive Obedience, you may find that a sport called Rally O is more to your liking.

This is loosely based on Obedience, and also has a few exercises borrowed from Agility when you get to the highest levels. Handler and dog must complete a course, in the designated order, which has a variety of different exercises that could number from 12 to

20. The course is timed and the team must complete within the time limit that is set, but there are no bonus marks for speed.

The great advantage of Rally O is that it is very relaxed, and anyone can compete; indeed, it has proved very popular for handlers with disabilities as they are able to work their dogs to a high standard and compete on equal terms.

## Flyball

This is a fast and furious sport, which is always accompanied by a huge amount of enthusiastic barking.

It is a team sport where four dogs are selected to run in a relay race against an opposing team. The dogs are sent out by their handlers to jump four hurdles, catch the ball from the flyball box and then return over the hurdles. The teams compete against the clock, and a heat is decided when the fourth dog crosses the finishing line.

The Cockapoo is a natural retriever, and if this instinct is encouraged early on with lots of play and reward, he will soon become ball obsessed, which is the key to a great flyball dog.

## Heelwork to music

Also known as Canine Freestyle, this activity is becoming increasingly popular. Dog and handler perform a choreographed routine to music, allowing the dog to show off an array of tricks and moves, which delight the crowd. This discipline demands a huge amount of training, but Cockapoos enjoy the variety that is involved, and cannot resist the opportunity to show off!

*Teaching tricks is a great way of spending quality time interacting with your Cockapoo.*

# |Health care

We are fortunate that the Cockapoo
is a healthy breed and, with good
routine care, a well-balanced diet,
and sufficient exercise, most will
experience few health problems.

However, it is your responsibility to put a programme
of preventative health care in place – and this should
start from the moment your puppy, or older dog,
arrives in his new home.

## Vaccinations

Dogs are subject to a number of contagious
diseases. In the old days, these were killers,
and resulted in heartbreak for many owners.
Vaccinations have been developed, and the
occurrence of the major infectious diseases is now
very rare. However, this will only remain the case
if all pet owners follow a strict policy of vaccinating
their dogs.

There are vaccinations available for the following diseases:

**Adenovirus:** (Canine Adenovirus): This affects the liver; affected dogs have a classic 'blue eye'.

**Distemper:** A viral disease which causes chest and gastro-intestinal damage. The brain may also be affected, leading to fits and paralysis.

**Parvovirus:** Causes severe gastro enteritis, and most commonly affects puppies.

**Leptospirosis:** This bacterial disease is carried by rats and affects many mammals, including humans. It causes liver and kidney damage.

**Rabies:** A virus that affects the nervous system and is invariably fatal. The first signs are abnormal behavior, when the infected dog may bite another animal or a person. Paralysis and death follow. Vaccination is compulsory in most countries. In the UK, dogs travelling overseas must be vaccinated.

**Kennel Cough:** There are several strains of Kennel Cough, but they all result in a harsh, dry, cough. This disease is rarely fatal; in fact most dogs make a good recovery within a matter of weeks and show few signs of ill health while they are affected. However, kennel cough is highly infectious among dogs that live together so, for this reason, most boarding kennels will insist that your dog is protected by the vaccine, which is given as nose drops.

Lyme Disease: This is a bacterial disease transmitted by ticks (see page 168). The first signs are limping, but the heart, kidneys and nervous system can also be affected. The ticks that transmit the disease occur in specific regions, such as the north-east states of the USA, some of the southern states, California and the upper Mississippi region. Lyme disease is still rare in the UK so vaccinations are not routinely offered.

## Vaccination programme

In the USA, the American Animal Hospital Association advises vaccination for core diseases, which they list as: distemper, adenovirus, parvovirus and rabies. The requirement for vaccinating for non-core diseases – leptospirosis, lyme disease and kennel cough – should be assessed depending on a dog's individual risk and his likely exposure to the disease.

In the UK, vaccinations are routinely given for distemper, adenovirus, leptospirosis and parvovirus.

In most cases, a puppy will start his vaccinations at around eight weeks of age, with the second part given a fortnight later. However, this does vary depending on the individual policy of veterinary practices, and the incidence of disease in your area. You should also talk to your vet about whether to give annual booster vaccinations.

# Parasites

No matter how well you look after your Cockapoo, you will have to accept that parasites – internal and external – are ever present, and you need to take preventative action.

Internal parasites: As the name suggests, these parasites live inside your dog. Most will find a home in the digestive tract, but there is also a parasite that lives in the heart. If infestation is unchecked, a dog's health will be severely jeopardised, but routine preventative treatment is simple and effective.

External parasites: These parasites live on your dog's body – in his skin and fur, and sometimes in his ears.

## Roundworm

This is found in the small intestine, and signs of infestation will be a poor coat, a pot belly, diarrhoea and lethargy. Pregnant mothers should be treated, but it is almost inevitable that parasites will be passed on to the puppies. For this reason, a breeder will start a worming programme, which you will need to continue. Ask your vet for advice on treatment, which will need to continue throughout your dog's life.

## Tapeworm

Infection occurs when fleas and lice are ingested; the adult worm takes up residence in the small intestine, releasing mobile segments (which contain eggs) which can be seen in a dog's feces as small rice-like grains. The only other obvious sign of infestation is irritation of the anus. Again, routine preventative treatment is required throughout your Cockapoo's life.

## Heartworm

This parasite is transmitted by mosquitos, and so will only occur where these insects thrive. A warm environment is needed for the parasite to develop, so it is more likely to be present in areas with a warm, humid climate. However, it is found in all parts of the USA, although its prevalence does vary. At present, heartworm is rarely seen in the UK.

Heartworm live in the right side of the heart. Larvae can grow up to 14 inches (35cm) in length. A dog with heartworm is at severe risk from heart failure, so preventative treatment, as advised by your vet, is essential. Dogs living in the USA should have regular blood tests to check for the presence of infection.

## Lungworm

Lungworm, or *Angiostrongylus vasorum*, is a parasite that lives in the heart and major blood vessels supplying the lungs. It can cause many problems, such as breathing difficulties, blood-clotting problems, sickness and diarrhoea, seizures, and can even be fatal. The parasite is carried by slugs and snails, and the dog becomes infected when ingesting these, often accidentally when rummaging through undergrowth. Lungworm is not common, but it is on the increase and a responsible owner should be aware of it. Fortunately, it is easily preventable and even affected dogs usually make a full recovery if treated early enough. Your vet will be able to advise you on the risks in your area and what form of treatment may be required.

## Fleas

A dog may carry dog fleas, cat fleas, and even human fleas. The flea stays on the dog only long enough to have a blood meal and to breed, but its presence will result in itching and scratching. If your dog has an allergy to fleas – which is usually a reaction to the flea's saliva – he will scratch himself until he is raw.

Spot-on treatment, which should be administered on a routine basis, is easy to use and highly effective on all types of fleas. You can also treat your dog with a spray or with insecticidal shampoo. Bear in mind that the whole environment your dog lives in will need to be sprayed, and all other pets living in your home will also need to be treated.

## How to detect fleas

You may suspect your dog has fleas, but how can you be sure? There are two methods to try.

Run a fine comb through your dog's coat, and see if you can detect the presence of fleas on the skin, or clinging to the comb. Alternatively, sit your dog on some white paper and rub his back. This will dislodge faeces from the fleas, which will be visible as small brown specks. To double check, shake the specks on to some damp cotton-wool (cotton). Flea faeces consist of the dried blood taken from the host, so if the specks turn a lighter shade of red, you know your dog has fleas.

## Ticks

These are blood-sucking parasites, most frequently found in rural areas where sheep or deer are present. The main danger is their ability to pass lyme disease to both dogs and humans. Lyme disease is prevalent in some areas of the USA (see page 163), although it is still rare in the UK. The treatment you give your dog for fleas generally works for ticks, but you should discuss the best product to use with your vet.

## How to remove a tick

If you spot a tick on your dog, do not try to pluck it off as you risk leaving the hard mouthparts embedded in his skin. The best way to remove a tick is to use a fine pair of tweezers or you can buy a tick remover. Grasp the tick head firmly and then pull the tick straight out from the skin. If you are using a tick remover, check the instructions, as some recommend a circular twist when pulling. When you have removed the tick, clean the area with mild soap and water.

## Ear mites

These parasites live in the outer ear canal. The signs of infestation are a brown, waxy discharge, and your dog will continually shake his head and scratch his ear. If you suspect your Cockapoo has ear mites, a visit to the vet will be needed so that medicated ear drops can be prescribed.

## Fur mites

These small, white parasites are visible to the naked eye and are often referred to as 'walking dandruff'. They cause a scurfy coat and mild itchiness. However, they are zoonetic – transferable to humans – so prompt treatment with an insecticide prescribed by your vet is essential.

## Harvest mites

These are picked up from the undergrowth, and can be seen as a bright orange patch on the webbing between the toes, although this can be found elsewhere on the body, such as on the ear flaps. Treatment is effective with the appropriate insecticide.

## Skin mites

There are two types of parasite that burrow into a dog's skin. Demodex canis is transferred from a mother to her pups while they are feeding. Treatment is with a topical preparation, and sometimes antibiotics are needed.

The other skin mite is Sarcoptes scabiei, causes intense itching and hair loss. It is highly contagious, so all dogs in a household will need to be treated, which involves repeated bathing with a medicated shampoo.

# Common ailments

As with all living animals, dogs can be affected by a variety of ailments. Most can be treated effectively after consulting with your vet, who will prescribe appropriate medication and will advise you on how to care for your dog's needs.

Here are some of the more common problems that could affect your Cockapoo, with advice on how to deal with them.

## Anal glands

These are two small sacs on either side of the anus, which produce a dark-brown secretion that dogs use when they mark their territory. The anal glands should empty every time a dog defecates but if they become blocked or impacted, a dog will experience increasing discomfort. He may nibble at his rear end,

or 'scoot' his bottom along the ground to relieve the irritation.

Treatment involves a trip to the vet, who will empty the glands manually. It is important to do this without delay or infection may occur.

## Dental problems

Good dental hygiene will do much to minimise gum infection and tooth decay, which is why teeth cleaning should be part of your regular care routine. If tartar accumulates to the extent that you cannot remove it by brushing, the vet will need to intervene. In a situation such as this, an anaesthetic will need to be administered so the tartar can be removed manually.

## Diarrhoea

There are many reasons why a dog has diarrhoea, but most commonly it is the result of scavenging, a sudden change of diet, or an adverse reaction to a particular type of food.

If your dog is suffering from diarrhoea, the first step is to withdraw food for a day. It is important that he does not dehydrate, so make sure that fresh drinking water is available. However, drinking too much can increase the diarrhoea, which may be accompanied with vomiting, so limit how much he drinks at any one time.

After allowing the stomach to rest, feed a bland diet, such as white fish or chicken, with boiled rice, for a few days. In most cases, your dog's motions will return to normal and you can resume normal feeding, although this should be done gradually.

However, if this fails to work and the diarrhoea persists for more than a few days, you should consult you vet. Your dog may have an infection, which needs to be treated with antibiotics, or the diarrhoea may indicate some other problem which needs expert diagnosis.

## Ear infections

The Cockapoo has drop ears, which may be medium or long in length, with varying degrees of feathering. The problem with ears of this type is that the air does not circulate as freely as when the ears are erect, and so there is an increased risk of ear infections.

A healthy ear is clean with no sign of redness or inflammation, and no evidence of a waxy brown discharge or a foul odor. If you see your dog scratching his ear, shaking his head, or holding one ear at an odd angle, you will need to consult your vet.

The most likely causes are ear mites, an infection, or there may a foreign body, such as a grass seed, trapped in the ear.

Depending on the cause, treatment is with medicated ear drops, possibly containing antibiotics. If a foreign body is suspected, the vet will need to carry our further investigations.

## Eye problems

The Cockapoo has large, round, well set eyes; there is no exaggeration, such as drooping eyes or prominent eyes, which may be vulnerable to infection or injury. However, in some cases, hair can grow too close to the eye, and this may need to be plucked to ensure that it does not come into contact with the eyeball.

If your Cockapoo's eyes look red and sore, he may be suffering from conjunctivitis. This may, or may not be accompanied with a watery or a crusty discharge. Conjunctivitis can be caused by a bacterial or viral infection, it could be the result of an injury, or it could be an adverse reaction to pollen.

You will need to consult your vet for a correct diagnosis, but in the case of an infection, treatment with medicated eye drops is effective.

Conjunctivitis may also be the first sign of more serious inherited eye problems (see page 182).

In some instances, a dog may suffer from dry, itchy eye, which he may further injure through scratching. This condition, known as keratoconjunctivitis sicca, may be inherited.

## Foreign bodies

In the home, puppies – and some older dogs – cannot resist chewing anything that looks interesting. The toys you choose for your dog should be suitably robust to withstand damage, but children's toys can be irresistible. Some dogs will chew – and swallow – anything from socks, tights, and any other items from the laundry basket to golf balls and stones from the garden. Obviously, these items are indigestible and could cause an obstruction in your dog's intestine, which is potentially lethal.

The signs to look for are vomiting, and a tucked up posture. The dog will often be restless and will look as though he is in pain. In this situation, you must get your dog to the vet without delay, as surgery will be needed to remove the obstruction.

## Heatstroke

The Cockapoo is built without exaggeration, and so is not prone to overheating and respiratory problems which can affect flat-nosed breeds, such as the Pug or the French Bulldog.

However, all dogs can overheat on hot days, and this can have disastrous consequences. If the weather is warm make sure your Cockapoo has access to shady areas, and wait for a cooler part of the day before going

for a walk. Be extra careful if you leave your Cockapoo in the car, as the temperature can rise dramatically - even on a cloudy day. Heatstroke can happen very rapidly, and unless you are able lower your dog's temperature, it can be fatal.

If your Cockapoo appears to be suffering from heatstroke, lie him flat and work at lowering his temperature by spraying him with cool water and covering him with wet towels. As soon as he has made some recovery, take him to the vet where cold intravenous fluids can be administered.

## Lameness/ limping

There are a wide variety of reasons why a dog can go lame - from a simple muscle strain, to a fracture, ligament damage, or more complex problems with the joints. If you are concerned about your dog, do not delay in seeking help.

As your Cockapoo becomes more elderly, he may suffer from arthritis, which you will see as general stiffness, particularly when he gets up after resting.  It will help if you ensure his bed is in a warm draught-free location, and if your Cockapoo gets wet after exercise, you must dry him thoroughly.

If your Cockapoo seems to be in pain, consult your vet who will be able to help with pain relief medication.

## Skin problems

The Cockapoo can be prone to skin problems; the skin appears to be more sensitive and rashes, sores and other irritations, are not uncommon. The causes are various and you will probably need a vet to help you pinpoint the reason.

Fleas, and other external parasites can result in itching, and the skin can become very sore and inflamed if the dog has an allergic reaction. Food intolerance and environmental factors, such as dust mites or pollen, can also cause major skin problems. For more information, see Skin Disorders, page 187.

# Breed-specific disorders

As a crossbreed, the Cockapoo is generally healthy. However, responsible breeders are aware of the prevalence of some breed specific conditions that may be inherited, and health testing of breeding stock is promoted by all the Cockapoo clubs.

## Eye disorders

### Hereditary cataracts

Cataracts are an opacification of the lens that tends to occur in older dogs. There are varying degrees of severity, the inherited form often having little effect on eyesight but, if necessary, surgery is usually successful.

## Progressive retinal atrophy (PRCD-PRA)

This is a bilateral degenerative disease of the cells (rods and cones) of the retina, caused by a defective prcd gene. The first signs are night blindness but it progresses to complete loss of vision. In most cases, the disease is first recognized in adolescence or early adulthood, and there is no cure. There is a test available for younger dogs, before being used for breeding, to prevent carrier individuals passing on the genetic defect.

## Familial nephropathy (FN)

This condition comes from show and working Cocker lines. Dogs are born with normal kidneys but because they lack a certain type of collagen, the kidneys start to deteriorate when a puppy is just a few months old, and this will often be associated with a slowing of the growth rate. As the disease progresses, the kidneys become increasingly less efficient in performing their task of waste disposal and the inevitable outcome is kidney failure.

Research should be undertaken to discover if this disorder has appeared in Cocker bloodlines before breeding is undertaken.

## Hip dysplasia (HD)

This is where the ball-and-socket joint of the hip develops incorrectly so that the head of the femur (ball) and the acetabulum of the pelvis (socket) do not fit snugly. This causes pain in the joint and may be seen as lameness in dogs as young as five months old with deterioration into severe arthritis over time.

In the US, hip scoring is carried out by the Orthopaedic Foundation for Animals. X-rays are submitted when a dog is two years old. In the UK, the minimum age for the hips to be assessed by X-ray is 12 months.

## Liver disease

This may take the form of chronic active hepatitis or copper toxicosis, and is becoming more prevalent in Cocker Spaniels. The pattern of inheritance is uncertain at present, but research into Cocker Spaniel bloodlines should be undertaken before a litter is planned.

## Patellar luxation

This is a condition where the kneecap (patella) slips out of place or dislocates. The kneecap moves in a groove at the lower end of the femur (thigh bone). Some dogs – mostly small breeds – are born with a groove that is not deep enough to retain the kneecap so that it pops out of place.

The characteristic sign is when a Cockapoo hops for a few paces, and then resumes his normal gait when the kneecap slips back into position. It is usually spotted in puppies when they are between five and ten months of age. Sometimes both legs are affected, and if the dog is also overweight, the effect can be crippling.

Surgery may be needed in severe cases but generally a Cockapoo will live with this condition and be largely unaffected, although arthritis may occur in the stifle in later life.

## Phosphofructokinase (PFK)

Phosphofructokinase is one of the most important regulatory enzymes of glycolysis, which is the foundation of respiration, both anaerobic and aerobic. A deficiency of phosphofructokinase, which is an inherited condition that can affect American Cocker Spaniels, is characterized by severe vomiting and muscle cramps in response to vigorous bursts of exercise.

This condition can be managed to a reasonable extent by playing close attention to activity levels. Again, breeding stock should be closely examined for evidence of this disorder in preceding generations.

# Skin disorders

As already highlighted, the Cockapoo has a sensitive skin and disorders may be the result of allergies to food, parasites or environmental factor. There are a number of breed specific conditions that should also be considered:

## Canine Atopic Dermatitis

This may be inherited, or it may be the result of a Cockapoo being exposed to an irritant over a period of time. Generally it develops in dogs aged one to three, and is seen as red patches on the skin (often the underarms and hindquarters) as well as on the paws, and results in biting and scratching of the affected area. Dogs can be treated with medication prescribed by a vet.

## Seborrhea

This is most commonly seen in Cocker Spaniels and predisposition to the disorder is passed on to Cockapoos.

The signs are a scaly skin, which my be wet or dry, which results in the skin flaking and hair loss. The causes are various: allergies, ringworm, metabolic disease, or it could involve the auto immune system. A vet will need to discover the underlying cause in order to prescribe effective treatment.

## Hypothyroidism

This is a condition where the body fails to produce a sufficient quantity of the thyroid hormone. The first signs you will see are weight gain and lethargy, and the affected dog may also suffer from chronic skin problems and hair loss. There is no cure, but it can be treated using a synthetic third hormone. Early diagnosis is key to successful management of this condition.

## Rage syndrome

Also known as Cocker Rage Syndrome, and perhaps more accurately as Sudden Onset Aggression, it has been seen in both English and American Cocker Spaniels but it has also been recorded in a number of other breeds. An affected dog will, without warning, make an unprovoked attack, often on a family member. After the attack the dog appears momentarily confused and then reverts to normal behaviour. The condition may be triggered by abnormal brain activity, as seen in seizures, but it is little understood at present. It does seem to be inherited so breeding stock should be closely vetted.

## Summing up

It may give the pet owner cause for concern to find about health problems that may affect their dog. But it is important to bear in mind that acquiring some basic knowledge is an asset, as it will allow you to spot signs of trouble at an early stage. Early diagnosis is very often the means to the most effective treatment.

Fortunately, the Cockapoo is a generally healthy and disease-free dog with his only visits to the vet being annual check-ups. In most cases, owners can look forward to enjoying many happy years with this loyal companion.

# Useful addresses

The Cockapoo Club of GB:
The Old Forge
Midville Lane
Stickney
Boston
Lincolnshire
Web: www.cockapooclubgb.co.uk

Cockapoo Rescue, Rehoming and Respite:
Email: Rescue@cockapooclubgb.co.uk

The Cockapoo Club of America:
Web: www.cockapooclub.com

Cockapoo Images:
Web: http://cockapoimages.blogspot.co.uk

## Australia
Australian National Kennel Council (ANKC)
The Australian National Kennel Council is
the administrative body for pure breed canine
affairs in Australia. It does not, however,
deal directly with dog exhibitors, breeders
or judges. For information pertaining to
breeders, clubs or shows, please contact the
relevant State or Territory Body.

## International
Fédération Cynologique Internationalé (FCI)
Place Albert 1er, 13, B-6530 Thuin, Belgium.
Tel: +32 71 59.12.38
Fax: +32 71 59.22.29
Web: www.fci.be/

## Training and behavior
### UK
Association of Pet Dog Trainers
Telephone: 01285 810811
Web: http://www.apdt.co.uk

Canine Behaviour
Association of Pet Behaviour Counsellors
Telephone: 01386 751151
Web: http://www.apbc.org.uk/

### USA
Association of Pet Dog Trainers
Tel: 1 800 738 3647
Web: www.apdt.com/

American College of Veterinary Behaviorists
Web: http://dacvb.org/

American Veterinary Society of Animal
Behavior
Web: www.avsabonline.org/

### Australia
APDT Australia Inc
Web: www.apdt.com.au

For details of regional behaviorists, contact the
relevant State or Territory Controlling Body.